Operation Fraso Leon

Supreme Strategy for Combating Lions

By
Andrew Agbaje
Juhani Juusola

Kingdom Publishers

Copyright© Andrew Agbaje and Juhani Juusola 2025

All rights reserved. No part of this book may be reproduced in any form by photocopying or any electronic or mechanical means, including information storage or retrieval systems, without permission in writing from both the copyright owners and the publisher of the book. The rights of Andrew Agbaje and Juhani Juusola to be identified as the authors of this work have been asserted by them in accordance with the Copyright, Designs, and Patents Act 1988 and any subsequent amendments thereto.

A catalogue record for this book is available from the British Library.

All Scripture quotations have been taken from the Amplified Classic and King James versions of the Bible.

ISBN: 978-1-916801-31-8

1st Edition 2025 by Kingdom Publishers, London, UK.

You can purchase copies of this book from any leading bookstore or at:
www.kingdompublishers.co.uk

Contents

Preface	7
Chapter 1 Critical manual for a victorious year	9
Chapter 2 Survival after encountering lions is predicated on the strategic ability to "keep"	18
Chapter 3 The variable in the skill of 'keeping' is man	26
Chapter 4 Boundary: A strategic combat doctrine for wrestling lions	32
Chapter 5 Watchfulness: A non-negotiable spiritual skill to combat lions	39
Chapter 6 Deliverance from trans-generational blindness: a watchful strategy to combat lions	48
Chapter 7 Return to the Holy Spirit - our insurance against rampaging lions	55
Chapter 8 Combating lions that silence destiny	61
Chapter 9 Have God's children become slaves? why do these lions roar at us?	67
Chapter 10 Lion-like combatant: a call to spiritual trench warfare	74
Chapter 11 Strengthening defense to launch attacks against lions	83
Chapter 12 Arise and war against the 'him' in the lion— the spiritual terrorist of life's wilderness	89
Chapter 13 The emergence of God's lion-like men	94
Chapter 14 The heart of lion-like men	100
Chapter 15 The emergence of the roaring bride of Christ	108
Chapter 16 Accurately diagnosing the enemy's roar	115

Chapter 17 With God standing by, any lion can be defeated   120

Chapter 18 Testimony qualifies us to face Goliath or Golion, but the brook provides the weapons to defeat him   130

Chapter 19 Breaking the teeth of lions (Goliath's curse)   134

Chapter 20 Goliath/Golion is dead   140

Preface

If we were on a battlefield and forgot we were in the midst of war, we would be a casualty in no time. Awareness, vigilance, skill and equipment are critical for survival. It is sad that we, as followers of Jesus, so easily forget that we are in a war—an invisible war, but a real one nonetheless. We are at war with vicious lions that seek to undermine the Glory of God in our lives and delight to defy the armies of the Living God.

For we wrestle not against flesh and blood, but against principalities, against powers, against the rulers of the darkness of this world, against spiritual wickedness in high places. (Ephesians 6:12 KJV)

When Christ declared the foundation of the Church in Matthew 16:18, he was not speaking about a sleepy, feeble, and jellyfish Church whose ranks are filled with ignorant and incapacitated men who are unable to stop the mouths of lions and repel the onslaught at the Gates of Hell. Rather, He spoke of a glorious Church whose defense system is well able to neutralize any missiles from the launchpad of Hell and whose attack force is like a fiery arrow piercing the hearts of lions, serpents, and scorpions, and any manifestations of Hades.

And I say also unto thee, That thou art Peter, and upon this rock I will build my church; and the Gates of Hell shall not prevail against it. (Matthew 16:18 KJV)

Behold, I give unto you power to tread on serpents and scorpions, and over all the power of the enemy: and nothing shall by any means hurt you. (Luke 10:19 KJV)

Contained in the chapters of this book are the loaves of bread and fishes that the Lord broke before us while we waited in his presence for 23 weeks as He taught our hands to war against the spiritual lions contending against the body of Christ. In these bi-weekly meetings hosted by Andrew Agbaje and co-hosted by Juhani Juusola alongside brethren across the globe, the Holy Spirit opened our eyes to several spiritual truths and warfare strategies tested and proven effective against lions seeking to steal, kill, and destroy.

It is our prayer that the Holy Spirit will use this book to equip the Church to be strong in the Lord and the power of His might; to lay hold of the weapons of our warfare and contend against every demonic lion seeking to defy the armies of the Living God.

Emmanuel Ebenezer

Chapter 1
Critical manual for a victorious year

And David said unto Saul, Thy servant kept his father's sheep, and there came a lion, and a bear, and took a lamb out of the flock: And I went out after him, and smote him, and delivered it out of his mouth: and when he arose against me, I caught him by his beard, and smote him, and slew him. Thy servant slew both the lion and the bear: and this uncircumcised Philistine shall be as one of them, seeing he hath defied the armies of the living God. David said moreover, The LORD that delivered me out of the paw of the lion, and out of the paw of the bear, he will deliver me out of the hand of this Philistine. And Saul said unto David, Go, and the LORD be with thee. (1 Samuel 17:34–37 KJV)

Who through faith subdued kingdoms, wrought righteousness, obtained promises, stopped the mouths of lions. (Hebrews 11:33 KJV)

There are certain elements that will not allow us to transfer from where we used to be to where we ought to be; those are lions. And for that reason, the Holy Spirit has unveiled that we must contend with lions. We need to contend with everything that has a lion-like spirit, lion-like characteristics, and a lion-like nature. A lion-like nature is predatory, devouring, imposing, threatening, and infuses people with fear and trepidation. We need to fight and wrestle against threatening situations and circumstances, in short, spiritual lions, in your place of work, family, or ministry, that typify a predator attempting to swallow a prey. This needs urgent attention because it is as serious as defeating this lion today, which equates to arriving at your destiny tomorrow.

How do we defeat the lions? By putting on the breastplate of righteousness, retaining the helmet of salvation, having our loins girded about with truth and our feet shod with the preparation of the gospel of peace, and having in our hands a shield of faith and the sword of the Spirit. With these tools, lions can never prevail. If any of that equipment is discarded by us because of the pleasures of this life or pressure from the society, it may make us susceptible to lions lurking in dark spots. The Bible says that men and heroes of faith, who moved the power of God in their generation, were not just obtaining promises or doing mighty things like subduing kingdoms, they also stopped the mouths of lions. For some of them (David, Samson, Daniel, etc), stopping lions was literal rather than figurative.

A lion is always interested in someone who carries the weight of glory and carries a destiny within himself or herself.

Those characteristics of lions that stand against a man and his glory, a people and their glory, a generation and their glory, and a family and its glory, need to be contended with before we can enter into the dimensions of the glory that heaven has prepared for us.

One's geographical location does not matter. Because if one's destiny is to arrive at the palace, even though today the individual resides at the refuse dump, appointment with destiny remains unchanged. When Joseph was thrown into the pit by his siblings, he was still destined to be on the throne. Being in the pit or prison was a temporal occupation because the enemy knew that if he could get it right, he would eventually arrive on the throne. That is the way we are. *"Greater is he that lives within you than he that lives in the world"* (1 John 4:4 KJV), and for that reason much more than you recognize yourself, Satan recognizes you. Not just because of who you are, but because of your specific appointment with destiny. Do not degrade yourself based on your present circumstances.

Remember, Jesus was less than two years of age when Herod decided to kill every two-year-old child in the city. Why? Because he heard that the King of the Jews had been born. The destiny of that child became a terror to an authoritative ruler, a very vicious and wicked man sitting as a despot and traitor. It is unprecedented how an infant's birth could rouse a mighty lion (Herod) launching him into a devastating massacre of innocent children. We should be aware that institutions can be instigated to frame up mischief against a person and enact unimaginable and ungodly legislations, simply because Satan understands that there is a destiny child in that locality. The Bible states unequivocally as a main theme in a victorious life curriculum.... *They stopped the mouths of lions.*

A lion that is not destroyed is a dangerous lion.

We don't render lions incapacitated simply by blocking their mouths with a face mask. No! We must eradicate lions altogether for the mouth to be stopped. We are going to contend with lions, fight in and for our families, fight against some friends, and some neighbors, not just physically but also spiritually. Satan knows 'if we don't stop this seductress or addiction, she or it will stop us', and we must not give an advantage to the enemy. Because the enemy is always very precautionary, the enemy always tries to be at an advantage, and the Bible says that *we should not be ignorant of the devices of the devil lest he takes an advantage of us* (2 Cor 2:11).

Our obligation is to "Keep" as God's responsible servants.

And David said unto Saul, Thy servant kept his father's sheep, and there came a lion, and a bear, and took a lamb out of the flock: And I went out after him, and smote him, and delivered it out of his mouth: and when he arose against me, I caught him by his beard, and smote him, and slew him. (1 Samuel 17:34,35 KJV)

"Thy servant". This looks like someone who is weak, and that is our current state: we are God's children, God's servants, and God's people. And it looks as if we are very small, all alone in the wilderness of life. Whether people are supporting us or not, whether alone, married, or single; anywhere we are on the surface of the earth, and if we are born again, we are God's servant. But, as a servant of God, you have an obligation. In this story, the Bible says that David, as a servant, was keeping his father's sheep, suggesting responsibility.

The enemy may not decide to wonder about us if we are irresponsible. The enemy may not decide to consider us relevant if we choose to satisfy ourselves with laziness. If we choose to be addicted to the pleasures of this life and waste our time, the enemy may aptly conclude that such addiction is self-limiting because we have created a self-imposed lion for our own life. So, there is no room for irresponsibility in our service to God. As God's children, we must be occupied with something eternally relevant because idleness is a risk of becoming the devil's workshop.

Redeeming the time, because the days are evil. (Ephesians 5:16 KJV)

Demons, Satan, principalities and power, and kingdoms of darkness are practically interested in responsible servants of God. Satan's obligation includes undertaking misery for whosoever is responsible for and towards the kingdom of God. Whosoever has the responsibility of the King's business, is Satan's primordial target.

The Holy Ghost reveals that a believer must attain a level of responsibility, and must learn how to keep their sheep. Our finances may be the sheep God wants us to keep. We should not squander hard-earned currency—hard-earned money that we have sweated and labored for on irrelevant things. We must be obedient servants and acquire the skill of keeping money. It's not every euro or dollar we invest because we are uncertain of the outcome of the investment. And many have come into financial ruin because they have taken certain calculated risks, and have ended up in spiritual, physical, and financial poverty; subjecting them to the mercy of mortal men. People who were supposed to be flying high and lending to nations are now borrowing because they failed to keep their financial sheep.

Are we responsible? We are supposed to keep our body as the temple of the Holy Ghost. For whatever excuse and reason, we went astray last year, the Holy Ghost is saying we must afford to be responsible. How about responsibility as an intercessor, supplicating for all men? What did we relinquish last year? What did we fail to keep? Well, Satan is not responsible for every negative predicament. Some of those predicaments are caused by our carelessness, for which we need repentance. But when we arrive at the place of responsibility, where we have made up our minds to fight and defend what God has put upon our hands, then the enemy will be interested. At the same time, the Lord God of heaven will also be interested to wrought great deliverance through us. It is counterproductive to engage in warfare if we are disqualified by our irresponsibility.

To engage the lion, we must put things in order.

We must set our lives in order, our houses in order, and our consecration in order, so that the glory of God can shine forth and so that angels can be deployed to wrestle with us. We don't want to waste our time screaming like Baal worshipers, no! We want to touch tangible power in the spirit realm.

We must learn how to possess our body in sanctification, holiness, and honour. We must learn how to sanctify our eyes from the evils that are on social media. We must learn how to disconnect ourselves from the trending events of this age and shut down the voices that distract us. We must learn how to keep our minds from wandering away from the things of God and how to de-occupy our minds from the things of this world. It is a divine and human partnership where we do our part and God will always do his part. No one should say that because they are bored, they can watch any movie. One may risk a catastrophic fall like David when he committed adultery with Bathsheba. He was supposed to be at the battlefield keeping his sheep. He was busy gallivanting on a balcony, and suddenly became a murderer and an adulterer in a moment. 2 Samuel 11:1-17.

If we do not know how to keep, then there is no point in engaging lions ourselves because we have not developed the capacity to fight lions.

What will be so precious in our life this year that the enemy will be looking for? What habit are we going to cultivate that will be so precious that Satan will take an interest in us? We must learn to stand alone, walk alone, stay alone with God. We must learn to come out from among them and be separate, says the Lord of Hosts, we must learn to disengage from every covenant with darkness, learn not to quench the spirit, and learn not to forbid speaking in tongues.

So [to conclude], my brethren, earnestly desire and set your hearts on prophesying (on being inspired to preach and teach and to interpret God's will and purpose), and do not forbid or hinder speaking in [unknown] tongues. (1 Corinthians 14:39 AMPC)

Are you a pastor? If so, you must learn to keep your flock, learn how to be observant, know when the enemy tries to invade the flock, always be on the alert. A pastor should be able to see things (discernment and spiritual insight) before they happen to the congregation. Nothing should be left to chance. The Holy Ghost will always give advanced knowledge. You must learn to pastor spiritually, not physically. A true pastor learns to walk in the spirit.

God is raising gladiators of Zion, men and women who can wrestle with God and wrestle with the enemy and subdue kingdoms. We must learn how to keep the presence of the Holy Ghost. attract the angels, sing in the Spirit, and make melody in our hearts to the Lord. We should not indulge in unhealthy eating habits that are dangerous to our health. Do we add so much salt to our food and eat a lot of sugar? We must change this pattern and learn how to keep our bodies healthy. How about addiction to eating pizzas, burgers, and fries? Let us repent of undisciplined eating habits.

Beloved, I wish above all things that thou mayest prosper and be in health, even as thy soul prospereth. (3 John 1:2 KJV)

We must learn how to eat vegetables, eat a balanced diet, stop eating carbohydrates all the time. Our diet needs to change. We must learn how to dress properly as a lady. Godly women are not supposed to be displaying their naked body parts and tempting men or aiding lustful imaginations. A combatant against lions cannot dress to seduce. We must learn how to keep our bodies holy. The same rule applies to men.

That every one of you should know how to possess his vessel in sanctification and honour; Not in the lust of concupiscence, even as the Gentiles which know not God: (1 Thessalonians 4:4–5 KJV)

Notes

Chapter 2
Survival after encountering lions is predicated on the strategic ability to "keep"

And David said unto Saul, Thy servant kept his father's sheep, and there came a lion, and a bear, and took a lamb out of the flock: And I went out after him, and smote him, and delivered it out of his mouth: and when he arose against me, I caught him by his beard, and smote him, and slew him. Thy servant slew both the lion and the bear: and this uncircumcised Philistine shall be as one of them, seeing he hath defied the armies of the living God. David said moreover, The Lord that delivered me out of the paw of the lion, and out of the paw of the bear, he will deliver me out of the hand of this Philistine. And Saul said unto David, Go, and the Lord be with thee. (1 Samuel 17:34–37 KJV)

There is something that anchors the possibility of victory; there is something that becomes the character on which the victory is conditioned. There is something that must be in place before the Spirit of God can descend upon a man, and that word is our ability to keep. Everything begins from there. Because if we do not know how to keep, we can never know how to fight. The desire to keep is the desire to retain, to conquer, and to defeat everything that threatens what we want to keep. It is the appetite for survival. Jesus was determined to keep the disciples by all means. He told the Father

And now I am no more in the world, but these are in the world, and I come to thee. Holy Father, keep through thine own name those whom thou hast given me, that they may be one, as we are. (John 17:11 KJV)

Jesus is the lion of the tribe of Judah, but He understood how to keep. How to keep is the condition for all the victories that we are going to encounter. Jesus understood the gravity of what was kept in his hands. He understood that He wasn't just raising disciples, he understood that they were the foundation of the kingdom of God on earth. These were the foundation of what God wanted to do on earth. He envisioned and understood the depth to which God wanted to use these disciples. And then He was willing to keep them, and He kept them jealously. If we lack the insight and understanding of what God has committed into our hands, we might be careless with them.

And David said unto Saul, Thy servant kept his father's sheep, and there came a lion and a bear, and took a lamb out of the flock. (1 Samuel 17:34 KJV)

David knew how to keep. He knew the numbers of the sheep that were in his charge and their coordinates. So, he understood that one sheep had suddenly gone missing, and his eyes saw the location of the attack. He knew the direction where the lion came from because he was not dozing, or snoozing off on social media. He had the unprecedented ability to be alert because he was focused on keeping the number of sheep that were delivered to him.

The condition of being alive is predicated on our ability to keep.

And as the king passed by, he cried unto the king, and he said, Thy servant went out into the midst of the pathway, and behold, a man turned aside, and brought a man unto me, and said, Keep this man, if by any means he be seen, then shall thy life be for his life, for else thou shalt be pay a talent of silver. And as thy servant was busy here and there he was gone, And the king of Israel said unto him, So shall thy judgment be, thyself has decided. (1 Kings 20:39,40 KJV)

A sobering situation occurred years ago on a battlefield. While soldiers tried to escape from enemy arrows and bullets, engaging their shields in such a hectic atmosphere, a man received a commission, and his commission was to keep. —a very strategic commission to keep.

Well, maybe we will say that man is the Holy Ghost. Amid the battle of this decade, let's consider that this decade began with COVID-19 in 2020, vaccination in 2021, and the war in Ukraine in 2022. We are still in the midst of the battle, and suddenly the Holy Ghost is turning aside and is telling us to KEEP something in the midst of the confusion on this globe, economic upheavals, recession, sorrow, pain, death, calamity, shame, reproach, fear, and apprehension. In the midst of all these nation-crippling events, here comes the supernatural Holy Ghost himself, turning to us and saying:

"Keep this man, keep this ministry, keep this family, keep these children, keep this destiny, keep this profession, keep this academic, keep this career, keep this money, and keep your health.".

Your sheep could be your family. The Holy Ghost could have placed you in charge of your family and then said, tend to this family just as David did in the wilderness. You could be the one God has used as a covering in that family, and God is saying, Take care of those sheep. A serious question emerges, how can we keep a man on the battlefield when we can die at any time?

The battle is not as fierce as our ability to keep. Our skill of keeping is what keeps us alive. If we lose that ability, we have lost our survival mode. It appears that the life of the man who is to keep another man will never be taken away as long as the man he is keeping is alive. That means to us, our deliverance and our safety are conditioned upon our ability to keep.

The man who turned aside, and delivered the man to another man was not worried about the safety of the man being given the charge to keep. That makes us think that that man was the Holy Ghost. The Holy Ghost is not worried about our demise. No, because He is able to keep us from falling. The Holy Ghost is not worried about our being disadvantaged; he is able to keep us from falling. He is not worried about what we are worried about. He is only concerned about the obligation He has committed into our hands.

Now unto him that is able to keep you from falling, and to present you faultless before the presence of his glory with exceeding joy, (Jude 1:24 KJV)

Come to think of it, all these things were happening on a battlefield. How and why did this man enter the battlefield and face this kind of predicament? It is because something about him is strategic. Because the same man who turned around to look at him could have turned to somebody else. But destiny calls upon him.

Well, you might be looking at your predicament today, and you are asking, "Why me, why me, why me?" It is not a predicament; you have been destined to keep. You have been destined to keep a life; to insure a life, to ensure longevity is granted to another life. It's about the lamb. It's about the sheep. And as long as the sheep are alive, you will be alive. If the lion is able to devour the sheep, you will die. It's just a matter of time. Because for every sheep or every lamb the lion takes away from the fold of David, the lion grows in audacity, stride, and viciousness.

But when you devour the lion, the lion loses his ability. Every territorial spirit that the lion represents becomes decimated simply because you challenged the lion that wanted to invade your own territory. On the other hand, should the lion be successful, it's going to be rung out as an announcement in the territory of the wicked ones saying, "Yes, we know how to devour and we are doing this strategically." And it's just a matter of time, David will be devoured too, and the destiny of David to be the king of Israel will be eradicated by a lion in the forest. And how would this downfall begin? One lamb after the other, one lamb after the other, and one lamb after the other. And it is possible for one lion to invite two lions the next time because the predatory lion now has more faith in victory than defeat.

...And as thy servant was busy here...(vs. 40)

This servant was foolish because if he had been wise he would have understood that any slight mistake would cost him his dear life. If the enemy comes and sabotages your children while you are busy watching Telemundo or Netflix, then your children are being taken away from you, and it's just a matter of time before you are down. David had maybe tens of sheep, yet he was not busy here and there. He was so strategically focused, he understood the skill of keeping. Hence, God could raise him to a point where he could keep an entire nation. The Bible says that God raised up David; He brought him out of the wilderness of life to lead Israel by the skillfulness of his hands.

So he fed them according to the integrity of his heart; and guided them by the skilfulness of his hands. (Psalms 78:72 KJV)

But this decade is a decade of severe danger, yet it's a decade of supernatural possibility because a set of people who know how to keep will emerge. The spirit of God is heavily investing in this verb, the word 'keep'. Because everything is dependent on it.

From the sheepfolds to the throne.

He chose David also his servant, and took him from the sheepfolds: From following the ewes great with young he brought him to feed Jacob his people, and Israel his inheritance. So he fed them according to the integrity of his heart; and guided them by the skilfulness of his hands. (Psalm 78:70–72 KJV)

The story of David began in the sheepfold. What he did in the forest qualified him to feed the nation, created a path in David's life, recommended him before the angels, and made God choose him to lead an entire nation. What he did with the sheep in the wilderness all alone qualified David as a man who could sit on the throne for 40 years. Apparently, David had acquired some skills in his hands instrumental to devouring a lion, bear, and ultimately Goliath. Later, David said, *"He teachest my hands to war." (Psalm 18:34 KJV)*

Be ready to lay down your life to keep.

Whosoever has this ability to keep will be ready to die. Jesus said, *For whosoever will save his life shall lose it: and whosoever will lose his life for my sake shall find it. (Matthew 16:25 KJV)*

It is a strategy of keeping, an ability to lose your reputation, to go against the rules of engagement, and an ability to ensure that everything can go down and collapse if only it will lead to the preservation of another life. Then you are ready to go in for it. That is the desire to keep, and it is written in scripture. Esther entered that hall of fame as she was ready to give her life for her nation Israel.

Then Esther bade them return Mordecai this answer, Go, gather together all the Jews that are present in Shushan, and fast ye for me, and neither eat nor drink three days, night or day: I also and my maidens will fast likewise; and so will I go in unto the king, which is not according to the law: and if I perish, I perish. (Esther 4:15,16 KJV)

We can consistently observe historical precedence that the ability to keep is an instinct that requires us to die to ourselves and be ready to die in the circumstances of life. Those who enter this supreme dimension never die because the ability to keep is also bidirectional, thereby keeping them as well.

Notes

Chapter 3
The variable in the skill of 'keeping' is man

And David said unto Saul, Thy servant kept his father's sheep, and there came a lion, and a bear, and took a lamb out of the flock: And I went out after him, and smote him, and delivered it out of his mouth: and when he arose against me, I caught him by his beard, and smote him, and slew him. Thy servant slew both the lion and the bear: and this uncircumcised Philistine shall be as one of them, seeing he hath defied the armies of the living God. David said moreover, The Lord that delivered me out of the paw of the lion, and out of the paw of the bear, he will deliver me out of the hand of this Philistine. And Saul said unto David, Go, and the Lord be with thee. (1 Samuel 17:34–37 KJV)

God has placed great things in our hands, and the Spirit of God has made us realize that part of those things includes our life, health, finances, ministry, children, family, opportunities, and everything else that has to do with us. It may be a study if you are a student, or it may be a job. Nonetheless, we must understand the skill and acquire the skill of how to keep these things.

We do not begin to look for the armor that is necessary for us to stand on the evil day. We have the armor ready before the evil day.

It is not so much about the lion. The lion already has its power; there's nothing we can do about it. The lion has its teeth, mouth, strength, and paws; those are constant. What is not constant, i.e what is variable, is the ability to keep what God has given us. Because our proficiency in the skillfulness in keeping will correspond to the victory we will have over the lion. If we acquire the skills sufficiently to keep, we can guarantee that we have the power to destroy every kind of lion. Why is that so? Because the Lord will always be with us. God is always constant. He has always been with the believers, and He will always be with them. Jesus said, *"...And, lo, I am with you always, even unto the end of the world. Amen." (Matthew 28:20b KJV)*

What is not constant is the ability of a believer to keep; to keep the word of God, to keep praying and watching. It is pertinent for us to acquire that same skill and understand how to fight this battle. Why? Because David told us in Psalms 18:34: *"He teacheth my hands to war, so that a bow of steel is broken by mine arms."* David was taught by the Holy Ghost himself how to execute judgment over lions, bears, Goliath, and the Philistines. He knew how to fight; he was taught by the Lord. Out of nothing, in singleness and loneliness, four hundred disadvantaged men relocated from the city to stay with him in the wilderness. David produced mighty men who did devastating wonders, and they were called the mightiest of the mighty. These mighty men attained a level of might that the scripture created their own platform eternally describing their exploits, for us to learn.

How did David arrive at that level of sophistication and impact?

It was because it began here while he was in the forest as a teenager. He began to learn the possibility of keeping, the strategy of keeping, how to watch, how to pay attention, and how to be skilled in having the coordinates of where the sheep are at a particular point in time, at night, and during the day, without any support. He acquired the skill of standing alone. Remember, this is the youngest of all the children of Jesse. None of his brothers was with him in this bush or this wilderness.

Why are you thinking that you are lonely? Why are you thinking that everybody has forsaken you? Why has that demoralized you? We've got to learn from David that he acquired the skill of how to stay alone in the wilderness of life and how to bring victory back home from the wilderness without any support. The power of God is able to deliver every lamb that you have out of the mouth of the lion. But it is predicated upon your skillfulness in keeping; your ability to keep.

Our primary instruction; to keep.

*And the Lord God formed man of the dust of the ground, and breathed into his nostrils the breath of life; and man became a living soul. And the Lord God planted a garden eastward in Eden; and there he put the man whom he had formed. And the Lord God took the man, and put him into the garden of Eden to dress it **and to keep it**. (Genesis 2:7,8,15 KJV)*

The Bible says that when God formed man and that man became a living soul, God did something else. God decided to plant a garden for the man. In the strategy of God, he creates a man and he creates an assignment; He creates a man and He creates an accommodation; He creates a man and then He creates a responsibility; He creates a man and He creates a destiny; He creates a man and He creates an occupation; He creates a man and He creates a career; He creates a man and He creates a ministry.

God planted a garden in a geographical location called Eden, and then he put the man that he had created there. Why?

And the Lord God took the man, and put him into the garden of Eden to dress it and to keep it. (Genesis 2:15 KJV)

To keep that garden!

That is a very serious matter. Can you imagine that for the very first man that was created into this world, the very first person that breathed as a human being, the breath of life on the surface of this earth, his primary instruction from God was to dress the garden and then to keep the garden? This does mean to us that the very first instinct that God puts into any man is the ability to keep.

And keeping means an invitation to fight.

Keeping is not a language of jokes, fun, carelessness or frivolity. God formed man and initiated man into the serious business of keeping.

What has God delivered into your hands? What has God commissioned you to keep? What has God instructed you to keep? Your garden may be your children. If you are a man, your garden may be your home. If you are a pastor, your garden may be your flock. If you are a single mother, your garden may be your children.

It doesn't matter where you are on the surface of the earth; as long as you are connected to the Adamic race, you are under an obligation to keep something. And that thing must be the garden, the lamb, or the sheep that God has delivered into your hand. And we do know that something went wrong, and Adam could not keep the garden. He was driven out of the garden. Why? Because disaster struck. The lion of darkness, Satan himself, found his way into the garden. In the garden, Satan came as a serpent and stung Eve, the wife of Adam, which means Adam failed to keep the garden.

Remember, the matter is not about how great a lion is nor how evil or devastating the snake might be; everything was predicated upon Adam and David's ability to keep. God created a man, put that man in the garden, and said, keep it. How we wish that Adam had taken that matter seriously. How we wish that Adam was as versatile and sensitive as David, but Adam let loose the command that was given to him. Adam became relaxed. And so the enemy came and struck a devastating blow that had to take Jesus Christ 4,000 years later to come and give His own life so that He might keep something for us.

If you lose your strategic ability to keep, the matter of the lion coming to assault the lamb may just be a foregone conclusion. Why? Because if the lion comes and there is no resistance, it is obvious the lion will come again and take away the remaining sheep, and nothing will be left.

Notes

Chapter 4
Boundary: A strategic combat doctrine for wrestling lions

And David said unto Saul, Thy servant kept his father's sheep, and there came a lion, and a bear, and took a lamb out of the flock: And I went out after him, and smote him, and delivered it out of his mouth: and when he arose against me, I caught him by his beard, and smote him, and slew him. Thy servant slew both the lion and the bear: and this uncircumcised Philistine shall be as one of them, seeing he hath defied the armies of the living God. David said moreover, The Lord that delivered me out of the paw of the lion, and out of the paw of the bear, he will deliver me out of the hand of this Philistine. And Saul said unto David, Go, and the Lord be with thee. (1 Samuel 17:34–37 KJV)

Truly speaking, the lion is mighty and very strategic. The lion never attempts to attack when it is so real to him or her that there's going to be a defeat. The lion attempts to attack when he has given a calculative overview of the situation and there is a strategic likelihood of victory. After a lion has made an adequate evaluation of the situation and the output suggests a possibility of defeat, the lion will wait for another time, postponing the attack.

Similarly, Satan, the old serpent, was a lion from the time of Adam, he's still a lion today, and he will be a lion tomorrow until Jesus comes. He's a roaring lion. He's not a quiet one. He's always roaring. Seeking whom he may devour. But our ability to understand the strategy of this lion will arm us with the reclusive knowledge of how to deal with his wiles because he's extremely crafty and full of demonic wisdom. *Be well balanced (temperate, sober of mind), be vigilant and cautious at all times; for that enemy of yours, the devil, roams around like a lion roaring [in fierce hunger], seeking someone to seize upon and devour. (1 Peter 5:8 AMPC)*

Setting up boundaries.

He said, *"And there came a lion"* (vs. 34). What does this tell us? It tells us of the possibility of a boundary, somehow, somewhere. No one comes if there is no door to enter. If there was no boundary around the pasture, around the sheep that David was keeping, the verb used here would not be applicable because there is nothing like 'a lion came'. No, it can't just passed by, and as he passed by a lamb fell into its mouth because there is no boundary. But when the lion broke through a boundary, it became an arrival; The lion came!

He that diggeth a pit shall fall into it; and whoso breaketh an hedge, a serpent shall bite him. (Ecclesiastes 10:8 KJV)

If we break the hedge, the serpent will bite. Why? Because it is commanded by the Authority that created the serpent that they should not pass a particular boundary. There is always a boundary for everything that God creates. Even the sea has an instruction not to overwhelm the earth permanently. When it loses that ability to hold its boundary, the entire world can be drowned in a few minutes.

When He gave to the sea its limit and His decree that the waters should not transgress [across the boundaries set by] His command, when He appointed the foundations of the earth— (Proverbs 8:29 AMPC)

Whosoever breaketh the edge, the serpent will bite him, which means it is possible for us to keep our boundary intact and to know when the lion arrives. If there is no boundary and every door leads into you, into your system, into your ministry, into everything, you will never know when the lion arrives. Every country has a boundary. Every city has a boundary. Every home should have a boundary. Every ministry should have a boundary. Every life should have a boundary. Every career should have a boundary. Every health should have a boundary. Every financial system should have a boundary.

Hast not thou made an hedge about him, and about his house, and about all that he hath on every side? thou hast blessed the work of his hands, and his substance is increased in the land. (Job 1:10 KJV)

If we are able to solidify our boundary, we will be able to know when the lion comes— when he arrives. If our boundary does not exist, there is no need to fight lions because there is nothing to defend. Far back in the book of Job, one of the oldest books in the Bible, Satan was busy negotiating for that hedge, for that boundary that the Holy Ghost had set around Job's life. That boundary was there as Job prospered.

He that hath no rule over his own spirit is like a city that is broken down, and without walls. (Proverbs 25:28 KJV)

We see here that there is a possibility of having a city that is broken down. It is possible that a city exists without a wall. And God, through the wisdom he gave to Solomon, was able to compare that with something. He said, He that had no rule over his own spirit is like a city without walls. That is a tragedy! If we do not have rule over our spirit, if we cannot control our own spirit, it is a waste of time contending against lions. This means we don't have wall; we are not disciplined enough to set a boundary around our lives. We are always yes, yes, yes people. We never say no because we are afraid of the faces of people. Such a person is like a city without walls, a recipe for a disastrous invasion of lions.

Becoming the boundary.

And I sought for a man among them, that should make up the hedge, and stand in the gap before me for the land, that I should not destroy it: but I found none. (Ezekiel 22:30 KJV)

Do we see the crisis that God came into? God was looking for just one man who would make up the hedge. The cities were without walls spiritually. Something has broken those walls down, and whenever there is a breaking down of that magnitude, the person (Satan) who has the agenda of stealing, killing, and destroying has full ground to execute his ministry.

"I sought for a man that should make up the edge, I sought for a man that should build again the wall of righteousness, I sought for a man that should establish the boundary of holiness, I sought for a man that should establish again the boundary of the fear of God, I sought for a man that should bring to pass the boundaries of holiness, purity of heart, and circumcision of the heart, I sought for a man that should be dogged and disciplined, I sought for a man that would be decisive." But God said, I found none.

As much as we are praying that we want God to set up a boundary for us— to set up a boundary for our houses, families, and nation— do we know that God is also interested in us becoming the boundary of God?

God wanted to destroy Sodom and Gomorrah. There was a boundary over Sodom and Gomorrah that the God of the heavens and earth could not cross, and his name was Abraham. And God said, Can I do anything without informing the boundary? Can I trespass? Abraham will hold me to ransom. *And the Lord said, Shall I hide from Abraham [My friend and servant] what I am going to do, (Genesis 18:17, AMPC).*

God created Abraham. God can do anything without Abraham, but He has so committed Himself to this boundary that He must inform him. Think about it. A man had risen to a position where he became a boundary for a nation and a civilization; he became a boundary for thousands of people.

Therefore he said he would destroy them-- had not Moses, his chosen one, stood in the breach before him, to turn away his wrath from destroying them (Psalms 106:23 KJV)

Can you imagine that something was written like this in the Bible? God said He was going to destroy the Israelites because they committed sin and went astray. God had made up his mind, and said, I'm going to destroy them. And then all of a sudden, a hedge came in the person of Moses, and Moses began to preach to God, saying: You have to repent of that evil, have you forgotten your covenant with Abraham? God said, "Moses, don't worry. I need to destroy these people, and I will set up a seed after you." Moses said, "God forbid, you need to repent of that." Here the Bible tells us, *"Had not Moses, His chosen, stood before him in the breach."*

Moses became a hedge that God was faithful to because he wanted to retribute judgment over iniquity. Moses, his chosen one, decided to launch himself into that bridge, became a barrier, and said, "God you cannot destroy the people because of their sins." God did not destroy the people. God did not permit the destroyer to destroy them. Why? Because Moses made up his mind to become the hedge. He became the defense system; he became the boundary. If God could listen to a voice like that in the Old Testament, do you know that you can become that voice today in this generation?

You can rescue a nation out of disaster. You can rescue a continent from demonic oppression. Because of you, God can avert the famine, the reproach, and the demonic evil that has been registered for a nation for a particular time of the year. Because of us, natural disasters, earthquakes, evil onslaught, pandemics, wars, rioting, economic recession, and outbreaks can be scaled back. We can become a boundary where the enemy's lions will not devour God's people.

Notes

Chapter 5
Watchfulness: A non-negotiable spiritual skill to combat lions

And David said unto Saul, Thy servant kept his father's sheep, and there came a lion and a bear, and took a lamb out of the flock. (1 Samuel 17:34 KJV)

The lions have been here before we were born, and they will continue to be here after we are gone, if Jesus tarries. We are fighting against perennial strategic lions whose habitation transcends earth into the spirit realm. We are fighting lions that sometimes we cannot see physically. Apparently, they have some power—power ceded to them by Adam, power that they had received from God Almighty. But they are our enemies, and these lions are responsible for the devastation of nations, families, and individual lives.

The purpose, vision, and mission of the lion are to make our lands desolate, to make the church (the family of God), a biological family, a joyful marriage void of joy and peace. The purpose of the lion is to make your mission fail, to make the ministry empty, and to drain the man off the anointing and grace of God. The purpose of the lion is to suffocate life out of any good thing. There is no victory without a battle. We don't sing a victory song if we have not engaged in any conflict. There's no triumph without a test, and there is no testimony without a test. Thus, if we want to devour the plans of lions and put them on the backbench, release, and relinquish their power, and bring them down to where they belong under our feet, we must first identify the strategy on how to keep.

Thy servant kept his father's sheep, and there came a lion and a bear and took a lamb out of the flock.

In the explanation of David, we see that David was fully aware of the situation. He had a safe, situational awareness of the workings of the lion. And the key point is there is watchfulness—the ability to watch. What was taken was a lamb. That tells us about situational strategic awareness. He didn't say it was a sheep, fowl, or goat, that was taken by the lion. He said he took a lamb out of the flock. Watchfulness!

Watching over boundaries.

Nevertheless we made our prayer unto our God, and set a watch against them day and night, because of them. (Nehemiah 4:9 KJV)

In Nehemiah's era, the boundary was broken down. Jerusalem became free for all. Every Tom, Dick, and Harry came to Jerusalem. It became a polluted city. It became a city of desolation. However, here comes Nehemiah; he took on the responsibility of keeping. In his mind, he said, "Jerusalem is precious to me; I have been delivered Jerusalem to keep in my generation." But when he tried to keep Jerusalem, he realized it was a battle of futility. Why? Because Jerusalem had no walls. You can't fight lions when there are no boundaries. Jerusalem had no walls, so he told the king he needed to go to Jerusalem.

Nehemiah needed to set up walls because he had a strong desire to recover and keep the city. And he knew he could not begin to keep a city when the city did not have walls. As soon as he began the wall-building project, the lions began to mock him. Sanballat, Tobiah, and the Arabians began to mock Nehemiah. They began to weary him with their words. They began to suffocate the atmosphere with their negative statements. Nehemiah continued because he understood the principle of boundaries. And he began to build the wall. But then he did something else.

Nevertheless, we made our prayer unto our God, and set a watch against them day and night, because of them. (Nehemiah 4:9 KJV)

He set a watch against them day and night. It is not enough to have a desire to keep. It is not enough to learn how to build a wall or how to set up a boundary. It is also critically important to know and acquire the skill to set up a watch over the boundary that you are building. Why? Because if you set up a wall and you go your way and you think, "Well, the wall will take care of itself", The next time you arrive, you will realize that your city has no wall anymore. It has been rooted out.

We are at war against watchful enemies.

Wherefore a lion out of the forest shall slay them, and a wolf of the evenings shall spoil them, a leopard shall watch over their cities: everyone that goeth out thence shall be torn in pieces: because their transgressions are many, and their backslidings are increased. (Jeremiah 5:6 KJV)

Come to think of it! The combination of a lion, a wolf, and a leopard watching over a city—the outcome is already decided. That's what the Bible says: anyone who tries to escape or break the siege will be torn to pieces. Do you know our enemies are watching us? We are the only ones who are not watching! Our enemies know how we go out and how we come in. We are the only ones that are so carefree. We don't mind, we don't care, we talk anyhow, we do anything, we go anywhere, we talk to anybody, we just open ourselves to anything, we communicate, we engage in all kinds of conversations, whether it concerns us or not; we are just everywhere. The enemy is busy watching.

For I heard the defaming of many, fear on every side. Report, say they, and we will report it. All my familiars watched for my halting, saying, Peradventure he will be enticed, and we shall prevail against him, and we shall take our revenge on him. (Jeremiah 20:10 KJV)

The Bible says familiar spirits, demons, and wicked men and women are busy watching for the place where we are going to miss our steps. Satan imparted them with the ability to watch. They have been watching since you were born. The enemy does not launch an attack if it has not properly undertaken a period of watching. We must pay special attention to this particular skill, watchfulness. Why? Whether you like it or not, your enemy is watchful. It is their skill. The enemies know they cannot take revenge if they have not acquired and utilized that skill of watching. So why do believers sleep, slumber, and snore in spiritual darkness and blindness?

Watchfulness: a divine combat strategy.

Set up the standard upon the walls of Babylon, make the watch strong, set up the watchmen, prepare the ambushes: for the LORD hath both devised and done that which he spake against the inhabitants of Babylon. (Jeremiah 51:12 KJV)

The principle of warfare is the same from one generation to another. This is why victories are eluding the body of Christ. We are fighting and combating lions aimlessly. We are just shouting and screaming like Baal worshippers disconcertedly. We don't understand that our God is a God of principle. We don't understand that God works strategically. God doesn't launch into a battle without a strategy, and the enemy also does not attack without a strategy.

We learn how to set a boundary, but we don't know how to maintain it. We don't know that it is not sufficient to only build a boundary but we also need to maintain it by watching it. This is because we know that any crack in the wall will allow the enemy to invade, and it may be a devastating situation. The Bible says, "Make the watch strong." How strong is your situational awareness? How strong is your watchfulness?

Set a watch over your tongue and set a watch over your eyes. If you browse anything on the internet, if you listen to all kinds of music, if you go to any website, or if you watch pornography, you are a serious target of lions, waiting to devour you.

The burden of Dumah.

The burden of Dumah. He calleth to me out of Seir, Watchman, what of the night? Watchman, what of the night? The watchman said, The morning cometh, and also the night: if ye will enquire, enquire ye: return, come. (Isaiah 21:11,12 KJV)

The burden of Duma is the burden of the Almighty God. Christianity has lost watchmen and watchwomen. Families no longer have watchmen and watchwomen. We just live for the flesh. We are only able to see what we can see physically and our decisions are based on earthly sight. We have no spiritual binoculars in the realm of the spirit resulting in great spiritual blindness.

He calleth to me out of Seir, Watchman, what of the night? Watchman, what of the night? (vs. 11)

Watchman, what of the night? Because it is written: *"While men slept, the enemy came"* (Matthew 13:25 KJV). You see, robbers don't come during the day; they come at night. Every evil is done at night; witches fly to the coven at night. Everything evil happens at night, when men are sleeping, and the Holy Ghost is saying, The Burden of Duma!

Well, thank God for this watchman. This watchman had something to say. This watchman was at his duty post. This watchman says, "What do you want to ask about the night? What do you want to inquire about the night? We are here. We refuse to sleep. The day is about to break; the night is coming. Enquire, ask us, and we will deliver to you what you want to hear. Return and come." This is the position we need to take. We need to be able to tell when the enemy is coming, when they are trying to play pranks with our boundaries, and when the wicked rise to manipulate us again.

Paul's final charge: Watch!

For I know this, that after my departing shall grievous wolves enter in among you, not sparing the flock. Also of your own selves shall men arise, speaking perverse things, to draw away disciples after them. Therefore watch, and remember, that by the space of three years I ceased not to warn every one night and day with tears. (Acts 20:29–31 KJV)

Paul the Apostle was traveling, and this was his final warning to these believers. Paul said, this is the reality; I know that after I have departed, grievous wolves shall enter in. They will break the barrier. He said, 'not sparing the flock'. Do you know that when the lions come, they don't spare anything? They come to destroy, to kill, and to steal. The lions come to sabotage our victory. And Paul the apostle said, "After my departing, these grievous wolves shall come." But do you know he was speaking figuratively? Verse 30 tells us, *"And also of your own self shall men arise."*

Unfortunately, these grievous wolves may be colleagues, friends, family members, siblings, in-laws, and parents. The grievous wolves are people who have been strategically positioned somewhere by the enemy to take away the glory of God from our lives. He said, after my departing, shall men arise. In verse 31, Paul said, *"Therefore watch."* It really doesn't matter how many grievous wolves are going to spring forth after his departure. He said the key is watchfulness. Therefore watch!

Are you fighting against your society? Are you fighting against a community of spiritual darkness? Are you fighting against neighbors and landlords who are trying to subjugate the glory of God in your life? Are you fighting against men and women who are demonic? Are you fighting against ungodly people? Are you fighting against or are you resisting the forces of religion that are contrary to Christ? Are you fighting against persecution? Are you fighting against spiritual wickedness in high places? Therefore watch! It doesn't matter the volume of the grievous wolves. It doesn't matter how much they have strategized to take your peace away, the Holy Ghost is saying the strategy to defeat them is watchfulness.

Notes

Chapter 6
Deliverance from trans-generational blindness: a watchful strategy to combat lions

And David said unto Saul, Thy servant kept his father's sheep, and there came a lion, and a bear, and took a lamb out of the flock: And I went out after him, and smote him, and delivered it out of his mouth: and when he arose against me, I caught him by his beard, and smote him, and slew him. Thy servant slew both the lion and the bear: and this uncircumcised Philistine shall be as one of them, seeing he hath defied the armies of the living God. David said moreover, The LORD that delivered me out of the paw of the lion, and out of the paw of the bear, he will deliver me out of the hand of this Philistine. And Saul said unto David, Go, and the LORD be with thee. (1 Samuel 17:34–37 KJV)

God is a God of strategy. God is a God of principle. The Bible says God is a God of order. *Let all things be done decently and in order* (1 Corinthians 14:40). When we jettison God's strategy, we bring ourselves into confusion and our scream at him which we call prayer is not effective because he always points us back to the very beginning.

W-A-T-C-H.

W - We watch our words; we watch our wishes.

A - We watch our action; we watch our attitude.
T - We watch our thoughts; we watch our time.
C - We watch our conduct, character, and the churches that we attend.
H - We watch our habits; we watch our habitation.

When we sleep, we lose the ability to watch. We lose the ability to set up a boundary and keep it defensible. We also lose the ability to keep anything within the boundary. And because of that, the enemy has the power to come, and then they have the time to sow, and they also have the time to escape. In a short moment, one spiritual sleep can destroy everything in life.

Ye are all the children of light, and the children of the day: we are not of the night, nor of darkness. Therefore let us not sleep, as do others; but let us watch and be sober. (1 Thessalonians 5:5,6 KJV)

This scripture is not talking about physical sleep; it's talking about spiritual sleep. So many are slumbering spiritually, folding their hands casually, and being taken away by every wind, every gossip, every news, and every commotion here and there, but they are not doing what God has ordained them to do. He said, let's not sleep; don't be careless spiritually because we are the children of the day! Every family is at war. Every congregation is at war. And therefore, this is the reason why we must watch. Just imagine if David was asleep when the lion came. The lion could have slayed him quite easily.

Consider and hear me, O LORD my God: lighten mine eyes, lest I sleep the sleep of death; Lest mine enemy say, I have prevailed against him; and those that trouble me rejoice when I am moved. (Psalms 13:3,4 KJV)

When the soul is spiritually blind, the enemy can plan to devastate. The roaring lion is always seeking, and going to and fro because the lion can see. You don't see a blind lion going up and down. No, a blind lion stays under a tree and remains still because he cannot see where he's going. The enemy we are fighting is very accurate in his vision, always going to and fro. The devil told God when he was talking about Job that Job's boundary should be collapsed.

And the LORD said unto Satan, Whence comest thou? Then Satan answered the LORD, and said, From going to and fro in the earth, and from walking up and down in it. (Job 1:7 KJV)

Why does he have that capability? Because he has eyes. It is possible for us to enter a dimension where our vision always keeps the enemy trembling. The enemy only rejoices where a man cannot see.

But their minds were blinded: for until this day remaineth the same vail untaken away in the reading of the old testament; which veil is done away in Christ. But even unto this day, when Moses is read, the veil is upon their heart. Nevertheless when it shall turn to the Lord, the veil shall be taken away. (2 Corinthians 3:14–16 KJV)

An entire country, the people of Israel, had a problem understanding the things of the Spirit. A veil came upon their faces at the time of Moses and has lingered for more than 3000 years after that experience. More so, many years after that experience. Paul was writing that the veil remained on their faces. It is a transgenerational blindness.

The forefathers in this verse of scriptures were blinded because of the experience of Moses, and the glory of God, and they commanded that Moses needed to use a veil over his face. From that moment, that veil that was physically over Moses' face became a veil in the heart of the next generation, and several scores of generations continued, and they retained the veil on their hearts until today. Unfortunately, many Israelites do not recognize that Jesus Christ, the Messiah, has already come because the veil still blindfolds the heart.

What a terrible thing that a veil was negotiated for by a generation, and it became a transgenerational tragedy. Something your parents did not fight may become a debacle for you, a point of your defeat. Always the Achilles heel, always the point in which you always buckle under duress. Why? Because the veil on the face of a generation became a veil in the heart of the subsequent generation. And Apostle Paul said there is a remedy: *"Nevertheless when it shall turn to the Lord, the veil shall be taken away."* What has kept the lion to keep on attacking this generation of people is simply because the veil has been perpetuated trans-generationally. Sadly, this veil is transmissible.

Because thou sayest, I am rich, and increased with goods, and have need of nothing; and knowest not that thou art wretched, and miserable, and poor, ***and blind****, and naked: I counsel thee to buy of me gold tried in the fire, that thou mayest be rich; and white raiment, that thou mayest be clothed, and that the shame of thy nakedness do not appear; and* ***anoint thine eyes with eyesalve, that thou mayest see****.* (Revelation 3:17,18 KJV).

Diagnosing the blindness of the Laodicean church age.

This was a message from Jesus to the church of Laodicea. And here is that message coming to us in this generation. Jesus said this church made the wrong diagnosis of their situation. They looked at themselves from a physical standpoint, and they felt like they were wonderful. From a physical standpoint, they were in affluence; they were wealthy; they were changing garments, had beautiful costumes, and a beautiful wardrobe. They had mansions. When they park their cars during their Sunday services, everywhere is saturated with the latest models of Toyota, BMW, Mercedes, and Volvo. You wonder, "Wow, these are God's people, and they have been blessed by all material blessings." But Jesus said, as much as that was true, it had nothing to do with their state in the spirit realm.

Jesus made them realize that the comfort they had and the physical possessions that they had acquired did not translate to spiritual possessions. If anyone is busy thinking, "Oh well, the only thing I have is just this ability to pray ", my friend, you are richer than the people in Laodicea. Jesus here made a stark diagnosis of these people's terrible conditions. And what did he say about them?

...and knowest not that thou art wretched, and miserable, and poor, and blind, and naked:

That is a paradox because they have a lot of goods. They give money to the poor. They are so wealthy. They have the largest cathedral in town. Everybody in the church is always well dressed and thousands of dollars are in the offering bag. And everyone is dancing and praising God. Maybe you are also part of that church of Laodicea. And everything is nice. Jesus looked from heaven, and He said, "What a wretched people!" Jesus said, "You are miserable, you are poor, you are blind, and you are naked." Can you imagine the diagnosis of Jesus? Does it make sense when you look at it from a physical standpoint that the most affluent churches in the world fit into the Laodicean category? Naked, blind, poor, wretched, and miserable.

Wealth and power, popularity, and political influence do not correspond to spiritual light, clothing, liberty, and spiritual vision.

They are two different things. And Jesus said, "Here is my counsel." Jesus began to tell them about the things they needed to acquire to be able to remedy the emergency state of their time. And concluded with, *"And anoint thine eyes with eyesalve that thou mayest see."*

Notes

Chapter 7
Return to the Holy Spirit - our insurance against rampaging lions

And David said unto Saul, Thy servant kept his father's sheep, and there came a lion, and a bear, and took a lamb out of the flock: (1 Samuel 17:34 KJV)

David had a dimension in his mind. He knows the coordinates of every lamb, and not a single lamb could be missed without understanding the geographical location of that lamb and what went missing. And he knew it was a lamb that went missing, not a sheep that went missing. And he went after the lion to secure the life of a lamb that was so feeble.

That lamb represented David's future as a shepherd because the lamb grows to become a sheep, and tomorrow that sheep will give birth to other lambs. Today it was a lamb, and that lamb was so weak. And the lamb's security and life were dependent upon the alertness, watchfulness, and vigilance of David. If David had been sloppy, that lamb would have died, and the future would have been extinguished. Thus, David took it upon himself to put his life on the line for an animal as small as a lamb. Why should such a man do such a thing? Why should such a man think that way? Why should such a man consider that something is greater than his life and worthy to fight for?

From the principle that David utilized, we cannot be surprised by his victory. Because it takes a man who has had an experience of God that think and apply things like David did. Let's consider one example of something that happened to David prior to this experience, what made David stand out, and why he was acting this way because this was foolishness to human reasoning, and rationale. But to the Spirit of God, that was wisdom.

"And the Spirit of the Lord came upon David from that day forward." (1 Samuel 16:13 KJV)

The Lion had not come at this time, but the Spirit of the Lord was upon David from that day forward. That was the same Spirit that was responsible for the victory in the wilderness. David utilized the capability of that Spirit to address the situation of king Saul at a time when demons were oppressing the king. Devils tormented King Saul's life, he was agitated and had mental troubles. He had all kinds of demonic infestations in his life and looked desperately for solutions, but David came to his rescue.

And it came to pass, when the evil spirit from God was upon Saul, that David took an harp, and played with his hand: so Saul was refreshed, and was well, and the evil spirit departed from him. (1 Samuel 16:23 KJV)

The officers in the palace considered David a great musician, but that was not David. It was the Spirit of the Lord manifesting himself through a vessel. It was by the Spirit of God that David played the harp that released Saul from the bondage and the oppressions of the unclean spirit. And the spirit of darkness departed from Saul when David played. It was by that same Spirit that David went into the wilderness to keep his father's sheep.

Keep the presence of the Spirit of God in your life intact.

David kept the Spirit of God intact in his life. David did not mess with the Spirit of God that came upon his life. The Bible says, *"The Spirit of God was upon David from that day forward."* There is no vacation in the Holy Ghost. We don't vacate out of his presence because the lion is just hanging around the corner, looking for whom he may devour. It is a demonic strategy of the devil—devilish, evil, sensual, and hellish—to devour at any cost, at any point in time, and through any means.

The Spirit of God that has come upon you, the glory of God that you have seen, and the presence of God you have encountered are the greatest preservations you can ever have if you surely keep them with you. It doesn't matter if you are in the palace or in the wilderness. That Holy Ghost will roar against any lion that comes your way.

Trusting in the Spirit's wisdom as we return to the Holy Spirit.

1 Kings 20:35,36 says...

And a certain man of the sons of the prophets said unto his neighbour in the word of the LORD, Smite me, I pray thee. And the man refused to smite him. Then said he unto him, Because thou hast not obeyed the voice of the LORD, behold, as soon as thou art departed from me, a lion shall slay thee. And as soon as he was departed from him, a lion found him, and slew him.

The Prophet needed a wound so that he could look like he was injured or like an injured soldier and so that he could effectively deliver his prophecy to Ahab. The first man killed by the lion was the man who disobeyed the prophet. The prophet needed to show that he was coming out of the war, but he couldn't inflict the wounds on himself. So, he met his neighbor and said, "Strike me, please." It was an instruction from God. God's instructions may seem foolish to us as men. The man may have thought, "Why do you want me to use a sword to cause an injury to your body?" And the prophet told him, "This is from God." In verse 36, he said, *"You disobey the voice of God."* I mean, he must have informed him that this message was from God. You know, as men, we think we are wise. We think we have more wisdom than God, so we look at the things of God as foolish. But if we remember 1 Corinthians 1:27, it says, *"But God has chosen the foolish things of the world that He might shame the wise; and God has chosen the weak things of the world that He might shame the strong."*

As you are being watchful, what word has God given to you? What word has been said to you that looks foolish? May we not be wise in our own eyes. May we not use our carnal minds to judge the things of God. May we not use our carnal minds to judge spiritual things because the carnal mind is enmity against God, for it is not subject to the law of God. We can't use our carnal mind to judge the instructions of God while we are being watchful.

Now the second point we see is disobedience. We read that it says in verse 35: *And the man refused to smite him.* That's disobedience. What was the consequence of disobedience? It was death, *As soon as thou art departed from me, a lion shall slay thee. And as soon as he was departed from him, a lion found him, and slew him.* In the book of Ephesians 5:6 it says, *"Let no man deceive you with vain words: for because of these things cometh the wrath of God upon the children of disobedience."* Don't think you are too righteous; don't think you are too holy. It is a spirit that can influence a

Christian. We should be watchful, and our eyes should be alert to that spirit of disobedience so that, as soon as we sense it, we cast it out.

Notes

Chapter 8
Combating lions that silence destiny

And David said unto Saul, Thy servant kept his father's sheep, and there came a lion, and a bear, and took a lamb out of the flock: (1 Samuel 17:34 KJV)

Moreover take thou up a lamentation for the princes of Israel, And say, What is thy mother? A lioness: she lay down among lions, she nourished her whelps among young lions. And she brought up one of her whelps: it became a young lion, and it learned to catch the prey; it devoured men. The nations also heard of him; he was taken in their pit, and they brought him with chains unto the land of Egypt. Now when she saw that she had waited, and her hope was lost, then she took another of her whelps, and made him a young lion. And he went up and down among the lions, he became a young lion, and learned to catch the prey, and devoured men. And he knew their desolate palaces, and he laid waste their cities; and the land was desolate, and the fulness thereof, by the noise of his roaring. Then the nations set against him on every side from the provinces, and spread their net over him: he was taken in their pit. And they put him in ward in chains, and brought him to the king of Babylon: they brought him into holds, that his voice should no more be heard upon the mountains of Israel. (Ezekiel 19:1–9 KJV)

This lamentation was speaking about the kings of Israel. As of the time this was written, it was applicable to the Jews. In the New Testament, it is applicable to us because we are the Israel of God.

Take up also a lamentation. Take up a posture in prayer. Take up a strategy to peep into the mystery that causes people's voices to be silent forever. The first mistake Israel made as a nation was to lay down among the lions. Israel became comfortable dealing with foreign heathen nations. You can become careless, forget your boundaries, and become very loose. We see this happening in the body of Christ today; we have become so open and so loose!

The nation of Israel laid down among lions (heathen nations). She was very free, that's what the church is doing today. We have forgotten our heritage, the scriptures and the foundations of wisdom, and we have become comfortable with the world, just like the nation of Israel was comfortable with the kings of the heathen lands. She broke her boundaries.

The Bible says that this first king became a young lion, and he learned to devour men. This was not what God had ordained for his people; this was not the way God wanted them to walk. This king became carnivorous, so he was devouring his people. He was devouring men. He had learned the ways of the Syrians who sacrificed their children; he had learned the ways of the heathen nations; he was not distinct; he was not separate from them. Growing up, all he knew was the ways of the Babylonians and the ways of the Syrians, and he began to manifest this same way. He did not walk in the way of righteousness, but he did evil in the sight of the Lord. This is the same thing the church of God is doing today! Daniel, in the land of Babylon, purposed in his heart that he would not defile himself and walk in the ways of the Babylonians. But the church today no longer cares about walking in the ways of righteousness.

Eventually, this king was captured and brought with chains into the land of Egypt. He was nurtured and raised up in the way of the devil, and so he could not outgrow the smartness of the devil. The nations set a pit for him when they saw he was becoming great. Pharaoh, who himself was a lion, grabbed him, took him in chains, and took him to the land of Egypt. Why? So that he could no longer have a voice. You see, this is a tragedy. This is a sad story. The Church of Christ must awaken so that this same fate does not befall us.

Now when she saw that she had waited, and her hope was lost, then she took another of her whelps, and made him a young lion. And he went up and down among the lions, he became a young lion, and learned to catch the prey, and devoured men.
(Ezekiel 19:5,6 KJV)

You see, we might have thought that this king would have learned from the errors of the other king, but no, he also walked in the way of the heathen nations. He did not separate himself from darkness; he did not walk in righteousness; he did not learn the ways of God; he did not submit to God. Rather he became a lion, and he also began to devour men. practice idolatry; he also began to practice the systems and the order of the heathen nations. If Satan is your master, he will never give you all his strategies because he will reserve some against you so when you want to rebel against him, he will be able to subdue you.

A demonic concentration.

Then the nations set against him on every side from the provinces, and spread their net over him: he was taken in their pit. And they put him in ward in chains, and brought him to the king of Babylon:

they brought him into holds, that his voice should no more be heard upon the mountains of Israel. (Ezekiel 19:8,9 KJV)

And here, the Holy Ghost explained to us by Ezekiel. He said, *"Then the nations set against him on every side from the provinces."* This is what we consider a demonic concentration. This is a demonic strategy whereby all nations set themselves against an individual. Then the question is this: why would the nations go to such an extent as to extinguish the light of just one person? It is because these nations understand the capabilities inherent in this individual. Do you know that it appears that believers are the ones who do not know who they are? But the nations know what God can do through you. And Satan also knows that if God keeps only one apostle alive, his kingdom will be wreaked with great havoc. And therefore, what does he do? He tries to extinguish that light as early as possible.

When Jesus Christ was born, about the age of two to four, suddenly there was a law in the kingdom that every child less than a particular age must be slaughtered. And an angel came and said, "Rescue this child and relocate to Egypt until I bring words back to you that those who are seeking the child's life have died." What was the enemy planning? He wanted to hang the salvation of man on the tree and kill it prematurely, but God intervened.

Message in tongues.

"Just as the young lion was shut out into the destiny of his own domain, of his own privilege, of his own jurisdiction, and he failed woefully, and then he was replaced by another lion who wanted to execute the same capabilities, the same mission statement of the previous generation having done much much better, yet he could not last because nations set themselves against him."

Sometimes a people or a generation still have a little bit of light, and they want to consolidate that light. They want to transmit it to their children. They want to transmit it to the next generation. In one way or the other, they have that flicker of light, and they are about to run with it. Suddenly, that light is extinguished by strange means. One, is because of a decision they made prematurely, either in marriage or in the places of work, in the churches or congregations they belong to. Unfortunately, that destiny and glory is extinguished, and they spend the remaining part of their years lamenting because they remember the fire they used to have. But now they realize that it looks like they can't do anything anymore. Time has passed, and they begin in their hearts to say, "Will the next generation be better?" Here we are today. If we look back in time, we realize that this scenario has been playing from one generation to another.

The enemies did something: *"They set against him on every side"*.

Samson was such a mighty man of God, a prince in Israel, whose voice should not be silenced. But Samson's voice was silenced in the so-called marriage to Delilah. The marriage was a "configured crafty marriage" by the Philistines. The Philistines deployed a woman into Samson's life, and they paid the woman with the intent that the woman might vex his spirit until she was able to discover the secret of his power. Eventually, Samson was tied in chains and incarcerated. He began to dance as a criminal before his enemies. Ah, thank God his hair grew again, and the vengeance for his lost eyes led to his premature death (Judges 16:23-31).

Notes

Chapter 9
Have God's children become slaves? why do these lions roar at us?

And David said unto Saul, Thy servant kept his father's sheep, and there came a lion, and a bear, and took a lamb out of the flock: (1 Samuel 17:34 KJV)

Is Israel a servant? is he a homeborn slave? why is he spoiled? The young lions roared upon him, and yelled, and they made his land waste: his cities are burned without inhabitant. (Jeremiah 2:14,15 KJV)

Is Israel a servant? God saw all the manifestations in the life of Israel, and one question popped up: *Is Israel a slave?* Why is there no difference between Israel and slaves? Why is Israel now categorized as a servant? God Almighty through the scriptures, asked a very serious question that also should be asked in this generation. The Bible says, "Is Israel a servant?" If God is asking a question; He is not asking to inquire. He is trying to bring you into a particular consciousness because He is the all-knowing God.

Is Israel now a servant? And the answer is 'no', Israel was not born a servant. God answered that question in Exodus 4:22, *"And thou shalt say unto Pharaoh, Thus saith the LORD, Israel is my son, even my firstborn."*

Therefore, Israel was not a servant. But Israel gave himself to slavery. Israel was not a servant, but a son. *"And the servant abideth not in the house for ever: but the Son abideth ever."* (John 8:35 KJV). But now God was asking: I never made him a servant. Why is he now a slave?

It was a question that astonished God Almighty Himself. If that was the Old Testament, how about the New Testament? *But as many as received him, to them gave he power to become the sons of God, even to them that believe on his name:* (John 1:12 KJV)

Our introduction into the kingdom of God is an introduction into sonship. We are conscripted into sonship in Christ, which means that because of that privilege, we have certain dispositions and characteristics. If truly we are being led by the Spirit in God's kingdom, there are peculiar manifestations that we need to see daily. They shouldn't be something so scarce, but something that is accustomed to our practice as believers. Because Jesus said,

And these signs shall follow them that believe; In my name shall they cast out devils; they shall speak with new tongues; They shall take up serpents; and if they drink any deadly thing, it shall not hurt them; they shall lay hands on the sick, and they shall recover. (Matthew 16:17,18 KJV)

These are the characteristics of people who are children of God, who are sons and daughters of God. And if we fast-track to 2 Corinthians 6:17,18 Paul the apostle said: *Wherefore come out from among them, and be ye separate, saith the Lord, and touch not the unclean thing; and I will receive you, And will be a Father unto you, and ye shall be my sons and daughters, saith the Lord Almighty.*

Now comes the question for us in this generation: is Israel a servant? Have we become servants? Have we been subjected to the vicissitudes of life? Have we become so hypnotized by our lackluster religiosity, a spirituality that has no reference to heaven, a spirituality that is only full of emotionalism and intellectualism? Have we become subservient to such kinds of principles? If the answer is yes, then the predicament that befell Israel has befallen us all.

The reason why God searched for Israel in Egypt was because they were taken captive, not willfully; Pharaoh decided and turned them into servants. God sought them because Israel was not born a slave. Israel gave herself to slavery by being attracted by the practice of the heathen, and then the young lions came after her.

Two evils.

For my people have committed two evils; they have forsaken me the fountain of living waters, and hewed them out cisterns, broken cisterns, that can hold no water. (Jeremiah 2:13 KJV)

In Jeremiah 2:13, God made a serious diagnosis. He said, *"For my people have committed two evils."* And now it is very rare for you to see in the Bible where evils in the plural are counted. It's very strange. Evil is supposed to be 'evil'. When they say evils then there's no need to count it. The Bible says, *"That by two immutable things, in which it was impossible for God to lie..."* (Hebrew 6:18 KJV); *"God hath spoken once; twice have I heard this; that power belongeth unto God."* (Psalm 62:11 KJV) Anytime God uses 'two' in the scriptures, it is an implication of finality and authenticity. And here the Bible says *"My people have committed two evils,"* so there is nothing else that could be committed that could fit into this category. Look at what God described as this finality of evil:

<u>Evil number one</u>: *"They have forsaken me, the fountain of living water."*

We didn't understand this until Jesus came to us to tell us in John 7:37-39:

In the last day, that great day of the feast, Jesus stood and cried, saying, If any man thirst, let him come unto me, and drink. He that believeth on me, as the scripture hath said, out of his belly shall flow rivers of living water. (But this spake he of the Spirit, which they that believe on him should receive: for the Holy Ghost was not yet given; because that Jesus was not yet glorified.)

Now Christ has been glorified, and here the Bible says the first capital evil that anybody, any Israelite, can commit is to forsake the fountain of living water, that is, to forsake the Holy Spirit. It is evil.

<u>Evil number two</u>: *"and hewed them out cisterns, broken cisterns, that can hold no water".*

They have replaced the Holy Ghost with something else; they've built cisterns that can hold no water. They now have another reservoir. Do you know the implications of that? The lion is going to roar and yell at us. But in our generation, what are these cisterns? People have replaced the Holy Ghost with watching drama, and Christian movies. You can spend six hours watching Christian movies, from season one to season ten, but just spending time with the Holy Ghost and 30 minutes of prayer is very tedious and difficult, and you start snoring. You are hewing to yourself broken cisterns that can hold no water. So many people are spending several hours every day on social media. These activities take time and effort and when they are done, there is exhaustion and tiredness, and the Holy Ghost has no place anymore.

Many people have replaced the voice of the Spirit, the water of life, i.e the Holy Ghost, with religiosity and ceremony. Imagine that in John chapter 7 it was written, *"In the last day, that great day of the feast, Jesus stood and cried, saying, If any man thirst, let him come unto me, and drink."* The question is, what was the feast meant for? People came to the feast; they stayed until day seven, or day 14, and yet they were still thirsty.

Friend, are you a member of a denomination, and you have been devoting your energy there? You participate in everything they do, and you know that irrespective of the time that you have spent there, there is still an insatiable desire in your soul. There is something lacking; the water of life is not there. Do not settle for such religiosity; that is not it. If you do so, you have committed the second evil.

The five mandates of the lions upon servants.

The young lions roared upon him, and yelled, and they made his land waste: his cities are burned without inhabitant. (Jeremiah 2:15 KJV)

1. They roared upon him. They roared to frighten Israel and make him afraid.

2. They yelled at him. When you yell at somebody, it means you have confidence that you can overpower him. So the young lions saw that Israel had departed from the living God and that they had broken the hedge. The church has gone into the way of religiosity. We are only after what we can do for ourselves, and the Spirit of God has departed. And now it's like the book of Revelation 3:20, *"Behold, I stand at the door, and knock: if any man hear my voice, and open the door, I will come in to him, and will sup with him, and he with me."* The Lord stands without, knocking for an open door.

3. *They made his land waste*. Every battle from the beginning of this world has been a battle for land or territory. Not just physical territory. Your land could be your ministry or the gift of God that He has given to you to manifest His glory. The reason why the young lions came after Israel was because they wanted to exert control and dominance over Israel's territory. Satan is not happy that your family is blossoming. He's not happy that your children are beginning to see the light of the gospel. Satan is not happy when he sees a standing church on fire for JESUS; he will try to dismantle it.

4. <u>They burnt his cities.</u> Israel did not learn how to keep the land that was filled with milk and honey. What happened? The lions came and ravaged the land because Israel did not learn to keep. So they wasted their years and their harvest. The king of Babylon enslaved them.

5. <u>They made his city desolate (without inhabitants)</u> so that nobody was there again. What used to be a glorious land suddenly became uninhabitable; nobody wanted to be there. Why? The glory had departed.

Our consecration to God must grow upward, not downward. Separation from the world and its practices is very essential to the manifestation of the glory of God.
Wherefore come out from among them, and be ye separate, saith the Lord, and touch not the unclean thing; and I will receive you, And will be a Father unto you, and ye shall be my sons and daughters, saith the Lord Almighty. (2 Corinthians 6:7,8 KJV)

Notes

Chapter 10
Lion-like combatant: a call to spiritual trench warfare

And David said unto Saul, Thy servant kept his father's sheep, and there came a lion, and a bear, and took a lamb out of the flock: And I went out after him, and smote him, and delivered it out of his mouth: and when he arose against me, I caught him by his beard, and smote him, and slew him. Thy servant slew both the lion and the bear: and this uncircumcised Philistine shall be as one of them, seeing he hath defied the armies of the living God. David said moreover, The Lord that delivered me out of the paw of the lion, and out of the paw of the bear, he will deliver me out of the hand of this Philistine. And Saul said unto David, Go, and the Lord be with thee. (1 Samuel 17:34–37 KJV)

My soul is among lions: and I lie even among them that are set on fire, even the sons of men, whose teeth are spears and arrows, and their tongue a sharp sword. (Psalms 57:4 KJV)

We can see from the above scripture that lions are everywhere around us in this world irrespective of our geographic location, there are always lions.

As if a man did flee from a lion, and a bear met him; or went into the house, and leaned his hand on the wall, and a serpent bit him. (Amos 5:19 KJV)

We can't escape lions; it's not an option. We need to fight against lions and to be able to do this, we need the necessary weapons from

God. 2 Corinthians 10:4, *"For the weapons of our warfare are not carnal, but mighty through God to the pulling down of strong holds."* We are not only supposed to be defending in this battle, but God has designed that we use the sword of the spirit in the epic part of this battle. We attack the lion before the lion attacks us, like David did; we use the sword of the Spirit. We must have the full armor of God while we walk around, and go into any place, even in our home. We must wear it every day, and we must wear it in prayer. Ephesians 6:18, *"Praying always with all prayer and supplication in the Spirit, and watching thereunto with all perseverance and supplication for all saints."*

Combating from the standpoint of Christ's victory.

The roaring of the lion, and the voice of the fierce lion, and the teeth of the young lions, are broken. (Job 4:10,11 KJV)

This was not speaking about the future. This speaks of what has already happened. And as we know from the scriptures, the Devil is like a roaring lion, going about, looking for whom he may devour. But we also know from the scripture that our Lord and our Savior Jesus Christ is called a Lion in Revelation 5:4,5, *"And I wept much, because no man was found worthy to open and to read the book, neither to look thereon. And one of the elders saith unto me, Weep not: behold, the Lion of the tribe of Juda, the Root of David, hath prevailed to open the book, and to loose the seven seals thereof."* So we see that the Lion of the tribe of Judah has prevailed! The teeth of the roaring lion (Satan) have been broken!

And you, being dead in your sins and the uncircumcision of your flesh, hath he quickened together with him, having forgiven you all trespasses; Blotting out the handwriting of ordinances that was against us, which was contrary to us, and took it out of the way, nailing it to his cross; And having spoiled principalities and powers, he made a shew of them openly, triumphing over them in it. (Colossians 2:13–15 KJV)

Everything portrayed in the above scripture is in the past tense; it has happened. This is our situation. By the death of our Lord Jesus Christ, the victory has been won. He has won the victory; He doesn't need to prevail again, but He has already prevailed. We are going to combat from the standpoint of victory, just like David went after the lion.

It takes a lion to defeat a lion.

And of the Gadites there separated themselves unto David into the hold to the wilderness men of might, and men of war fit for the battle, that could handle shield and buckler, whose faces were like the faces of lions, and were as swift as the roes upon the mountains. (1 Chronicles 12:8 KJV)

It takes a lion to defeat a lion. Every lion is connected to a particular tribe or genealogy. And we know that we are connected to the lion of the tribe of Judah. Therefore, we are from Zion, distinct from the enemy that is going about ravaging homes and families. God wants us to know that we are lions. And as lions, we have a duty. The Gadites had their faces like the faces of lions, and their countenance was like the countenance of lions. In fact, any man who looks at any of the Gadites will simply describe them as, "These men are lions, men of courage, boldness, zeal, power, and of great might."

These were not characteristics obtained by people who folded their hands casually. These men literally looked like lions. Why? Because they have been carrying out activities that have configured them to look like lions. These men were men of war and were attracted to

David in the wilderness because they had the same kind of spirit. Jesus is the Lion of the tribe of Judah. Our countenance will begin to change into His own image because of our interaction with the Holy Spirit.

We must also begin to take responsibility because lions are territorial in nature. Lions are hungry for territories. We are made to conquer the enemy's territories. Just as we are lions for the kingdom of God there are also other lions going from place to place, devouring souls. When we understand that we are lions, we will realise that we are made to claim territories for God. The first thing Jesus said when he resurrected after the disciples met him was: *"Go therefore and make disciples of all the nations, baptizing them in the name of the Father and of the Son and of the Holy Spirit,"* (Matthew 28:19 KJV). In other words, Jesus said they should go and take territories for His Kingdom by winning lost souls, healing the sick, casting out devils, and setting the captives free!

The Gadites dimension.

And of the Gadites there separated themselves unto David into the hold to the wilderness men of might, and men of war fit for the battle, that could handle shield and buckler, whose faces were like the faces of lions, and were as swift as the roes upon the mountains. (1 Chronicles 12:8 KJV)

These men of Gad separated themselves. Capacity and potential existed within those people. The Bible says, *"And of the Gadites, they have separated themselves unto David into the hold to the wilderness."* They did not go to the palace or evening parties. They went into the hold, into the trench, forest, and wilderness. Importantly, a relocation from the city's comfort into the wilderness of uncertainties. This is not a call to everybody; this is a call to certain people who have certain capabilities. And what were their capabilities?

The Bible says they were described as men of might and men of war who were fit for the battle. They were described as men who understood or had the skill of handling spears, shields, and bucklers. They were described as men whose faces were configured, reconfigured, and metamorphosed into the faces of lions. They were described as men who were fast and swift, like rows on the mountains. Men with these strategic characteristics and levels of potential are people to whom we should ask two questions.

Question one. Were they born like this? The answer is no. How did they get themselves to this point? Which battles did they think they were going to fight in their future that they so armed themselves to the teeth? They learned how to run, they learned how to throw spears, they learned how to change the contours of their faces and their appearance, they learned how to appear so fit at any point in time, and they were ready for emergencies. What inspired these men to create a possibility of this kind so that God could use them at any time? They were altogether available.

Question two. Having attained this level of capability, why shouldn't they stay in the city? The answer is this: they recognized that the capacity that God had built into them was not meant for the city. It was meant for the forest. It was made for the battleground. In the city, there are no battles. In the city, there is enjoyment, sleeping, cinema, drama, theater, and football, there is great comfort. In the forest, there is none of those things. There is no electricity, water, or light —nothing. Hard times. Those men understood that the skill that had been acquired so far was useless to the city because there was no war there.

Some people began accumulating spiritual strength. They began handling shields and bucklers. They understood the skill of handling the sword of the spirit. They knew how to preach the gospel, having their feet shod with the preparation of the gospel of Christ. They knew how to pray and how to wrestle in prayer. They were suddenly becoming the Gadites, with faces that were so versatile, and volatile like the faces of lions. However, with time, they settled on a denomination. They settled into being ushers, just wiping dust from the church benches. These are people who have capabilities; these are men who need to separate themselves into the wilderness. These are people that the Holy Ghost had so prepared. And because of their absence in the strategic battlefield stations where they ought to be, there is a defeat to the body of Christ. That's why we are—weak.

We are the only ones that can dispel the darkness, but where are the lion-like men? They are resting in the city; they are enjoying the sauna; they are enjoying the cake and coffee; they are relaxing in the theater; they are relaxing on social media; they are in the stadium watching football. For this reason, the church is defeated. For this reason, we do not see our signs. For this reason, the world mocks us and they ask us, "Where is our God?"

A call to spiritual trench warfare.

And of the Gadites there separated themselves unto David into the hold. (1 Chronicles 12:8a KJV)

The Bible says the Gadites separated themselves into the hold. There are many things that could typify the hold today. This does not imply that we physically go and dig a trench at the back of our house and say that we are fighting for the Lord. That's not what the scripture is talking about. In 1 Samuel 17:20, when David was coming to greet his brethren, the Bible says, *"and he came to the trench."*

The scripture could have said, "he came into the host". No, David was making his own personal observation of the geographical location. He came into the trench. At the time he came into the trench, the Israelites were on their way to the battle. So he came into the trench. If there is no trench where you are, please depart from the place. You are only a companion to those who can show you their trenches of prayers and Bible studies. You can only engage in long conversations with those who have trenches like you. Let your desire and your decision be transformed.

David's father sent him to his brother, but he was looking for a trench. The Bible says that after David had observed that there was a trench, he became familiar with the environment. There are places where you cannot stay for 30 minutes if you do not find your trench because a trench is a place that makes you feel at home. When David found the trench, he felt at home. What was the next thing? There was a great cry from his belly. He shouted for the battle. There was joy inside his spirit. You know in Psalm 122:1 David said, *"I was glad when they said unto me, Let us go into the house of the Lord."* He was not talking of a place where God is not, where God cannot be found. He was talking of a place where the Shekinah glory abounds.

So when you meet people, relate with them, and you cannot find trenches in their lives, and you are still busy laughing with them, it means you are dead spiritually. That's what it means. And you need resuscitation before it is too late because there is only a window, a golden chance of life, where "CPR" needs to be used for it to be effective. Otherwise, it will be too late. Many believers have landed in spiritual mortuaries, embalmed till Jesus comes. Why? Because they went into denominations that have no trenches.

One trench that we can separate ourselves into is evangelism. It is a trench. Because in evangelism, we wrestle against principalities. We plunder hell to populate heaven. We snatch men from the jaws of hell and push them into heaven. It is colossal warfare. That is why the Bible says that as part of our weapons of war, our feet are shod with the preparation of the gospel of peace. Friends, there are trenches all around us. You must launch yourself into this trench, and there you will see God manifest his power.

Notes

Chapter 11
Strengthening defense to launch attacks against lions

And David said unto Saul, Thy servant kept his father's sheep, and there came a lion, and a bear, and took a lamb out of the flock: And I went out after him, and smote him, and delivered it out of his mouth: and when he arose against me, I caught him by his beard, and smote him, and slew him. (1 Samuel 17:34,35 KJV)

Responsibility to keep: our first line of defense.

The scriptures began by saying David was trying to tell King Saul why he was qualified to fight Goliath. The first thing David had to convince Saul of was the strategy of his defense that he had accumulated over the course of days, months, weeks, or years. He said, *"Thy servant kept his father's sheep."* The Spirit of God taught us that in combating lions, we must have the desire to keep what God has committed into our hands. Now we, as believers, God may have committed something into our hands. It could be a talent, a grace, a spiritual gift, an anointing, an auction, a ministerial capability, an office, an assignment, a group of persons, or a disciple, we are responsible for keeping that thing. That is the first line of defense.

It is not everything we keep. There are many things God did not commit to our hands. There are many things ancestors commit in people's hands. There are many things cultural practices, ethnic groups, and society might have committed to our hands. Those are not the things to keep. The only thing that we are committed to keeping is what God has committed to our hands.

Setting boundaries around the obligation to keep: our second line of defense.

"And there came a lion and a bear..."

When you say something came, that means that thing arrived. That means that that thing crossed the boundary; that means there was a landmark that demarcated the frontier, a community, a territory. So when something enters that territory, that thing came, it arrived. If there was no landmark, then there is no coming, i.e., there is no arrival. This means not only did David learn in the wilderness how to keep, but he also learned how to set boundaries around the obligation to keep. He set boundaries around the sheep, He set boundaries around his own life. When the enemy came to take what belonged to David, that enemy got crushed against David's boundary.

If our life does not have boundaries, we will not even know when the enemy arrives. We will not know because we will just assume that 'it is still part of our boundary'. If you do not allow the Holy Ghost to create a boundary around you, you might even be fraternizing with a lion, and you are not aware that the adder and the viper are just your tenants. We don't just allow anything from every Tom, Dick and Harry. We don't just accept or open our hearts to any information. We are very sensitive and selective. There are things we don't hear, there are things we don't watch, there are books we don't read, there are videos we don't pay attention to, and there are conversations we don't engage in.

Because when the enemy wants to come, he must cross a fence. The Bible says, "Whoso breaketh an hedge, a serpent shall bite him." (Ecclesiastes 10:8 KJV) The strategy to keep what God has committed into our hands is a defense mechanism. The strategy to set a boundary reinforces the defense mechanism. Hence, we must understand that in our combat against lions, we must have a solid defense mechanism as well as a pivotal attack mechanism.

Watchfulness: our third line of defense.

...and took a lamb out of the flock: ...

That was watchfulness. David did not mistake the identity of the animal that entered jeopardy, which means he was watchful. No matter if it was at night, twilight, dark, dusk, dawn, or whatever time of the day it was, and whatever day it was when the lion invaded his boundary, David was in a vantage position. David was standing in a place where his vision was not clouded. He could identify and pinpoint without a Google map what was lost, where it was lost, and what was taken... David was watchful. That was the third strategy of defense.

He understood that it was not a sheep that was taken, but a lamb. Before we enter the attack mode, we've got to solidify our defense system: our defense system of watchfulness, our defense system of setting up boundaries, and our defense system of learning how to keep.

Strengthening every feeble and paralytic defense system in preparation for an attack.

Wherefore lift up the hands which hang down, and the feeble knees; And make straight paths for your feet, lest that which is lame be turned out of the way; but let it rather be healed. (Hebrews 12:12,13 KJV)

There is no negotiation for an epileptic, paralytic defense system. "Wherefore lift up the hands which hang down." What does that tell us? Imagine a man without hands, a man who has suffered a stroke, or a man whose hands are paralyzed. How can that man build up a defense? It is not possible. But do you know that in the realm of the spirit, there are many Christians whose hands are paralyzed? Because this was written to believers, there are many Christians going around with this kind of morphology, and with this kind of appearance. They only have mouths to talk in the physical realm, and they are empty spiritually. They are very light. Their hands are hanging down.

"And the feeble knees."

You need a knee that is strong to set up a defense system. In the book of Ephesians, chapter 6, many times Paul kept saying, *"And having done all these, stand."* Stand against the watch of the enemy. Your ability to stand is an indication that you have a fortress. If you don't have a fortress, then it means that are not standing. If you don't have a fortress, it's an indication that your knees are feeble. If you don't have a fortress, it's an indication that your hands are hanging down.

"Make straight path for your feet."

It is your feet. You must create a path for them. If there is no path for your feet, then the enemy will create a path for you. Why? Because as long as you have the feet, you must, of necessity, need a path to engage the feet. Except you want to cut off your feet, unfortunately, every person living on the surface of the earth has feet, physically and spiritually. Since there are feet, there are paths; there is a road that you have to walk in and walk on. And if you don't create that strength in your feet, the enemy will create a pathway for you that God does not want.

Notes

Chapter 12
Arise and war against the 'him' in the lion—the spiritual terrorist of life's wilderness

And David said unto Saul, Thy servant kept his father's sheep, and there came a lion, and a bear, and took a lamb out of the flock: And I went out after him, and smote him, and delivered it out of his mouth: and when he arose against me, I caught him by his beard, and smote him, and slew him. (1 Samuel 17:34,35 KJV)

"...And I went out after him."

It is very important that we discern our enemy. Who are we fighting? Before David got up, David immediately diagnosed the capabilities of the enemy, who the enemy is, and the nomenclature of the enemy. David knew who he wanted to fight and for what purpose. The Bible says that David said, *"And I went out after him."* David didn't call the lion "it'; he called the lion "him". That means the lion was a personality.

Every time the scripture referred to the lion, the Bible wrote it as "him", but in verse 35, the Bible says that when David smote him (that's referring to the lion), he delivered it (referring to the lamb). So that is the appropriate pronoun for an animal. You call an animal "it"; you don't call it "him" or "her". It's not a human being. The Bible used the right pronoun for the lamb as an animal that is natural. But throughout this verse, almost eight times, the Bible described the lion and the bear as "he", "his", and "him". It was by this same token that David talked about Goliath because he understood that it was not about fighting animals alone. He recognized that the 'him" that was slain in the lion who was rendered homeless jumped upon a bear, was rendered homeless, and entered Goliath. In this passage, the Bible talks about the spirit in an animal that was wrestling against David, and you will realize that the pattern of this approach had to be a pattern of spiritual intelligence.

Stepping out of your comfort zone to address the enemy's invasion.

David said, *"And I went out."* That is authorization because of the capabilities he had. He went out of what? He went out of his boundary. He went out of his zone of security. He went out of his comfort zone. He went and stepped his foot across the battle line. **You must be able to come out.** That is, after you have ensured that your defense is impenetrable; there is nothing important for you to stay inside doing when your defense is already assured. You know you can always fall back because God is behind you. David understood that, *well, there are other sheep —maybe 50 here —but I will go out of this fold and I will address the enemy that has invaded my territory.* Therefore he went out against the lion.

It was the same way the "him" entered the serpent and deceived Eve. It was not a problem with the snake; it was a problem with the devil that used the mouth of the snake to deceive Eve; Adam fell, and all of us entered a spiritual crisis. *But I fear, lest by any means, as the serpent beguiled Eve through his subtilty, so your minds should be corrupted from the simplicity that is in Christ. (2 Corinthians 11:3 KJV)*

In the same light, the "him" recognized that Samuel had anointed David to be king over Israel. The "him" had an idea that there is a root of Jesse that is in the future of the tribe of Judah until Shiloh comes. And he has seen that David appears to be the one after the heart of God who will maintain that lineage until Jesus comes. Thus, the "him" (that's Satan) entered and possessed a lion to try to kill David. David's father did not send him to go and die in the wilderness, but the aura and atmosphere around David meant a terror to the "him" that ruled the wilderness.

Here, David said, *"And I went out after him,"* which means that he came, took the lamb, and went away. The Bible says, *"The enemy came, sowed tares and went his way." (Mathew 13:25 KJV)* David was so deliberate, observing the pattern, the footsteps, and the direction the lion went with the lamb. First of all, David diagnosed that he was not dealing with just a physical lion; he would have used his rod for that. But he needed his hands for this!

David noted in scriptures that, *"He (God) teacheth my hands to war, so that a bow of steel is broken by mine arms" (Psalms 18:34 KJV).* David understood where the power was in his physical body; he knew that his hands were anointed. He had the speed to keep up with the pace of a lion. A man who carries the glory of God is a man who is given supernatural speed. What men cannot accomplish in years; you can do in a day because the Spirit of the living God rests upon you. By the same Spirit, David ran to meet Goliath. He didn't run backward when Goliath was coming; David ran to meet him.

The shout of the King.

He hath not beheld iniquity in Jacob, neither hath he seen perverseness in Israel: the LORD his God is with him, and the shout of a king is among them. (Numbers 23:21 KJV)

How do lions in the physical realm mark their territory? Once in a while, they let out a roar from the bottom of their belly, and every animal in the jungle trembles acknowledging, "The king is here." How do men know that the Holy One of Israel dwells within you if you don't have a shout within you? You're always praying "gentlemanly" prayers. When the day of Pentecost came, gentleman Peter, who could not stand the damsel, became a roaring lion. Everybody in Jerusalem heard them. They were in a tiny room, yet everybody heard them. What kind of noise were they making? There was no amplifier. The shout of the King entered them, and their bellies could not contain it anymore. They only let out a little bit, and as the shout was coming out of their lips, Jerusalem could not contain it.

A man with a shout of the King is not discouraged, depressed, disappointed, debilitated, diseased and bedridden. Circumstances do not knock your feet out of the way. No, why? Because there is a shout of battle. Wherever you see a trench, you are happy. Do you know that David didn't hear the roar of the lion because the shout inside of him was louder? Do you know that? When Goliath was rattling and he was saying many things, David didn't hear him as if he understood what he was saying. David was busy waiting for his turn to let out his own shout because, all the while, he was only listening to the shout inside of him.

Notes

Chapter 13
The emergence of God's lion-like men

And of Gad he said, Blessed be he that enlargeth Gad: he dwelleth as a lion, and teareth the arm with the crown of the head. And he provided the first part for himself, because there, in a portion of the lawgiver, was he seated; and he came with the heads of the people, he executed the justice of the Lord, and his judgments with Israel. (Deuteronomy 33:20,21 KJV)

In verse 20, *"Blessed be he that enlargeth Gad: he dwelleth as a lion..."* scripture didn't say he dwells like a lion. It said, *"He dwelleth as a lion."* So Gad was a very territorial tribe; because of God's enlargement, Gad dwelt as a lion. What is God trying to tell us here? When God is through with fashioning us in the place of prayers, we shall emerge as lions, not resembling lions, but as lions. *"And teareth the arm with the crown of the head."* When Israel was on their way to the promised land, the tribes of Gad and Reuben stopped before the river Jordan and took possession of their lands. They chased out the occupants and took over. God is expecting us to emerge so we can conquer the evil and wickedness in our world, set free those who are oppressed, and displace Satan from territories so we can lose those who are tied down by sin and Satan.

"And teareth the arm with the crown of the head." Arm speaks of power. What did the tribe of Gad do? Gad destabilized powers that existed even before he was born. Paul entered a city (Athens), and when he saw that the whole city was given to all kinds of idolatry and

pleasures, his spirit was moved within, and then he began to contend against the evil powers (Acts 17:16-34). God does not engage in an incomplete project. God does comprehensive work and if any man will release himself to God, and say, "God please have me completely". God will begin to enlarge that man, strengthen him as He strengthened David, and claim territories for Jesus through him.

Our emergence as lion-like men is hinged on our ability to dwell long in prayers till we encounter God.

Gad, a troop shall overcome him: but he shall overcome at the last. (Genesis 49:19 KJV)

A troop was destined to overtake Gad, but by virtue of this declaration of Moses, he dwelt as a lion. A people that was supposed to be trodden upon and overtaken, but by reason of God's enlargement, dwelt as a lion. The question we ask ourselves today is: Are we dwelling as lions? Are we coming from backgrounds that were destined to be oppressed? Some of us come from backgrounds that are full of negative and oppressive stories. But God is giving us a charge to dwell with Him in the place of prayer. How can we emerge if we don't pray? How can we emerge as God's lion-hearted men if we don't know God who is the lion of the tribe of Judah? How can God impart in our spirit a portion of Himself if we don't submit ourselves to him? If we don't take prayers as a lifestyle.

And Gad walked with God; the tribe of Gad followed Moses, and they followed the instructions of God which necessitated Moses' declaration. He said to Gad, from this day on, you shall dwell as a lion. How can we liberate the souls of men that have been bound by darkness and devils? Bondage such as pornography, masturbation, homosexuality, unclean thoughts, gambling, drugs, murders, etc are rampant. Others in their search for a solution have been initiated into the kingdom of darkness via new-age spirituality, mediation, yoga practices, etc. We are to launch out with power, with a lion's heart, contending against the darkness in the lives of men.

Divine provision is encapsulated in the Gadites' dimension; they will never live in poverty.

And of Gad he said, Blessed be he that enlargeth Gad: he dwelleth as a lion, and teareth the arm with the crown of the head. And he provided the first part for himself, because there, in a portion of the lawgiver, was he seated; and he came with the heads of the people, he executed the justice of the Lord, and his judgments with Israel. (Deuteronomy 33:20,21 KJV).

Verse 21, describes the result of Gad's entering into the dimension of his tribe by ordination because verse 1 stated it was the decree of Moses, the man of God, over the tribes of Israel. Therefore, this was an ordination and a divine commission, a prophetic utterance that came upon the tribe of Gad. What does this ordination entail? Gad will never live in poverty, be in want, or suffer the lack of anything good. This means that when we are conveyed into this dimension, there is a prepared provision attached. How many believers are struggling today? Was Elijah, the son of Tishbite, not part of this tribe? There was a famine in the land. God compelled a raven to feed him supernaturally. A raven does not play with meat, but a raven had to obey the order because a man of the spiritual tribe of Gad had arrived and needed to eat.

And the Bible says, *"He provided the first part for himself."* Do you remember when Elijah told the woman, Please make food for me first? The woman was trying to make food for herself and her child. And Elijah, the man of God, said, "No, make for me first." Why? Because he had the anointing for provision and multiplication. The

Gadites operate by the same principle, receiving provision first for themselves.

"Because there, in a portion of the lawgiver, was he seated; and he came with the heads of the people, he executed the justice of the Lord, and his judgments with Israel." This means that, as a result of the provision he had, Gad could not be dismissed from the hierarchy of events in society. Thus, when decisions are made in society, the Gadites must be present; otherwise, nothing will be done. In summary, there are provisions, placements and positions in Gad's tribe. The Bible says: *He raiseth up the poor out of the dust, and lifteth up the beggar from the dunghill, to set them among princes, and to make them inherit the throne of glory: for the pillars of the earth are the LORD'S, and he hath set the world upon them.* (1 Samuel 2:8 KJV)

Commission to execute God's justice and judgement is captured in the Gadites' dimension.

"And he came with the heads of the people, he executed the justice of the Lord, and his judgments with Israel."

This is tremendous power, that Gad can stand on behalf of God. Jesus was an embassy of God on the surface of the earth. When Jesus entered cities, demons cried, *"Why have you come to torment us before it is time? (Matthew 8:29 KJV).* Do we recognize that when Jesus crossed over the sea, He met at the portion of the Gadarenes, a man that the enemy had tied up? The man had the potential to bring the judgment of God upon the civilization of his day, but Satan said, No, this lion will not roar. More than 6,000 demons were in this man of the Gadarenes, tying up the lion in him. And Jesus came like Moses, the man of God, and set that man free from all the demons that had tied him up. And when that man was free, he emerged into Decapolis and began to execute the judgment of God upon sin and iniquity. And many were turned to the Lord; the evangelist in him began to roar (see Luke 8:26–39).

Notes

Chapter 14
The heart of lion-like men

Gad, a troop shall overcome him, but he shall overcome at last. (Genesis 49:19 KJV)

This was Jacob blessing all his children shortly before he died. Jacob was a patriarch; a man who had attained a certain hierarchy in heaven; he was a very hefty man in the spirit realm carrying a weight of glory. Whatever he pronounced stuck upon the people. Even though he was a natural man, he was also a spiritual man. The Bible says he looked at the tribe of Gad and told them that the beginning of their lives will start with a defeat, and then they shall overcome. Do you know that that is how all of us began when we were under the power of darkness in sin and iniquity? We were overcome by Satan, and he was the lion roaring and tormenting us until Jesus came. Hebrews chapter 2 says Jesus broke the power of sin, defeated Satan, and put him in prison so that we might be released. He blotted out handwriting written against us, which was contrary to us.

The unfortunate thing in this story is that between Genesis and Deuteronomy, it looked as if that tribe was fulfilling the first part of the prophecy of Jacob. Defeat. They were being overcome by the circumstances of life. When Jacob blessed Gad, he didn't stop at the tragic part of the story. He said, *"But he shall overcome at last."* It took several years— even hundreds of years. At this time, they were in Egypt when Jacob made this pronouncement. Do you remember that they spent 430 years in Egypt? And it was Moses that came to bring them out. For 400 years the Gadites were under the supreme utterance of Jacob that they would be overcome, they then walked another 40 years in the wilderness, resulting in 440 years of a suffocating pronouncement of their natural father.

But after 440 years, a man who was also hefty in the spirit realm but not of a natural lineage, Moses, the great prophet, now began to speak over the tribes, and in his speaking over the tribes, he altered what was spoken over Gad. He opened the charter of the second part of the covenant of God over Gad. For 440 years, Gad was living with a mentality of defeat, living as a slave, and was subjected to every circumstance of life, but a man of God, with a different dimension of anointing and a different glory, came and altered that eternal truth that was spoken over Gad. It doesn't matter how long the first part of the Gadites' life has been; when Moses uttered his own words, the tribe of Gad updated their credentials and identities.

Transformed from being overcome to "Dwelling as Lions".

And of Gad he said, Blessed be he that enlargeth Gad: he dwelleth as a lion, and teareth the arm with the crown of the head. (Deuteronomy 33:20 KJV)

Can you imagine that? Moses began by pronouncing blessedness over God. This is diametrically opposite to the way Jacob blessed Gad. Jacob blessed Gad by starting with the negative part of the blessing. But Moses altered the dimension, and he began to release blessings. And the blessedness of Gad proceeded thus, whereby he said, Gad, shall dwell as a lion because he shall be enlarged. That means prior to this time he was not enlarged; he was struggling, just barely living.

And of the Gadites there separated themselves unto David into the hold to the wilderness men of might, and men of war fit for the battle, that could handle shield and buckler, whose faces were like the faces of lions, and were as swift as the roes upon the mountains; (1 Chronicles 12:8 KJV)

And look at the characteristics of this tribe. The Bible said this tribe was no longer shy; the tribe of Gad changed into a tribe that had something to offer, no longer being liabilities. They came to David with their characteristics; men of might and fit for the battle. It is so fitting that the Holy Ghost said, that their faces were like those of lions. They had a different kind of heart. When the Bible talks about their faces, it is referring to their hearts, a transformation in the heart had occurred.

The heart of the matter is the matter of the heart.

And David said to Saul, Let no man's heart fail because of him; thy servant will go and fight with this Philistine. And Saul said to David, Thou art not able to go against this Philistine to fight with him: for thou art but a youth, and he a man of war from his youth. (1 Samuel 17:32,33 KJV)

This scripture tells us that David perfectly understood the language of spiritual warfare. David was an astute professional in spiritual warfare. He needed to educate the king of his country about what is most important in spiritual warfare. The most important thing in spiritual warfare is not the mind, soul, or flesh; it's the heart or spirit. The Bible says David gave a lecture to his king, the commander-in-chief of the armed forces of Israel, the five-star general; a lecture that the king did not understand.

He said, *"Let no man's heart fail."* David understood that when the lion came from the forest, the lion was looking for his heart to fail. But when he got up and ran after him, the lion turned to him because the lion was surprised at the audacity and effrontery of David in pursuing it. The language of the heart can only be gotten by those who walk in the Spirit. David lectured King Saul, the basic rudiment of spiritual warfare, and he said, *"Let no man's heart fail because of him."* Goliath understood that language because Goliath had been speaking for 40 days, and every sound of his voice sent the generals into the foxhole. Generals were hiding in caves; their armament, skills and weapons, were rendered useless because their hearts had failed.

Do you realize that in the matter of the civilization of the spirit realm, all the things you are accumulating and paying attention to will become insignificant if they do not build the strength of the heart? The soldiers of Israel were supercharged with the intellectual ability of how to use the sword and shield, how to throw the javelin, etc. They knew those skills, but now the battle they were fighting was not the battle of the physical equipment; it was the battle of the heart. *And Saul said to David, Thou art not able to go against this Philistine to fight with him: for thou art but a youth, and he a man of war from his youth* (1 Samuel 17:33 KJV). Saul could not diagnose the spirit that was in David. Saul could not understand that a boy, even though he's a youth, has the heart of a lion. He didn't know. Why? Because he does not have what it takes to know. Do you know that many people are misdiagnosing you? And yet you are running to them for validity. Many people don't know what you carry, and yet they are looking at you as if you don't have anything, and you are listening to them. My friend, you've got to change your audience.

God is interested in releasing into our civilization men and women with enlarged hearts. Men and women whose hearts will not fail. Men and women who are focused on God deliberately and diligently, and who will count the wisdom of this world as foolishness. Men and women who will so seek the face of God until God settles upon their lives. Men and women who will be called for emergencies, and they will respond. God is looking for youth, for young people who are willing to put their lives on the line and say, I will die for a cause. God is looking for those whose hearts will be sealed by the Holy Ghost Himself. God is looking for those who are naturally impotent; naturally, they don't have the weapons of war. Naturally, they are not equipped with spears and shields. Naturally, they don't have all the intelligence of military warfare, but spiritually, they are giants. That was what David had. Only HEART – A heart that cannot fail.

A heart that had been tested and tried by the lion, bear, and premature death. yet he didn't die. That was the heart that came to the battlefield. The Bible says that out of the abundance of the heart the mouth speaks (Luke 6:45 KJV). What kind of heart do you have? It forms your language and your vocabulary. The content of your heart is what you speak. If you have the mind of God and the heart of Elohim, you will speak his language. You will act on the basis of the constituent of your heart.

Spiritual men exuding lion-like boldness.

And David said unto Saul, Thy servant kept his father's sheep, and there came a lion, and a bear, and took a lamb out of the flock: (1 Samuel 17:34 KJV)

What does it mean to be spiritual men? God wants us to be people with hearts full of courage. That's why the Bible says, *"Have not I commanded thee? Be strong and of a good courage; be not afraid,* neither be thou dismayed: for the LORD thy God is with thee whithersoever thou goest" (Joshua 1:9 KJV). In life, if you don't have the lion's heart, you can never take the lion's share. The Bible says that the righteous are as bold as a lion (Proverbs 28:1 KJV). It takes righteousness to activate that lion-like level of boldness. The unrighteous are not bold; they panic and fear.

We must understand that our calling in God is to be people who will exude the fragrance of the Spirit, the attributes of the Holy Spirit, and the courage of the Spirit of the living God. The lion came after the sheep. David was not timid; he was not afraid. Automatically, David was instantly clothed by the Spirit of the living God. He had gotten to a point where God wanted us to reach. It takes boldness and courage to dismantle the works of darkness. In addition, strength in the heart is critical. The day of adversity came to David unexpectedly but the Bible says, *"If thou faint in the day of adversity, thy strength is small"* (Proverbs 24:10 KJV).

Now when they saw the boldness of Peter and John, and perceived that they were unlearned and ignorant men, they marvelled; and they took knowledge of them, that they had been with Jesus. (Acts 4:13 KJV) The disciples entered a certain dimension of boldness, and when the council saw them, they concluded that they had been with Christ. This is what God is expecting from us in this generation—nothing less.

MESSAGE IN TONGUES: *There is a transformation. There is an emergence. There is the rising up of God's army. There is the raising up of God's children. The world shall know it; men and women all over the world shall see it.*
They shall behold the rising of the elect. They shall behold the rising of the sons of God in this time. They shall behold the rising of those who God has called for this end time, for the time that we are in this

world. They shall behold the rising of the sons of God and the daughters of God, and the children that God has ordained to do damage, to do harm to the kingdoms of hell. And while the world goes down in depression, in darkness, in sickness, in turmoil, in disarray, these men and women who have given themselves to God; these men and women who have given themselves to the Spirit of God; these men and women who do not look at the obstacles, at the challenges; these men and women who do not look at the difficulties and the pains and the agonies in their world; these men and women who do not look at the obstacles of their background; these men and women who do not look at the powers contending against them, shall emerge. They shall shine as light in this dark world. They shall shine as light in the darkness of their world. And by that time, the Lord shall come; it's very close, says the Lord.

Notes

Chapter 15
The emergence of the roaring bride of Christ

That he might present it to himself a glorious church, not having spot, or wrinkle, or any such thing; but that it should be holy and without blemish. (Ephesians 5:27 KJV)

And as he talked with them, behold, there came up the champion, the Philistine of Gath, Goliath by name, out of the armies of the Philistines, and spake according to the same words: and David heard them. And all the men of Israel, when they saw the man, fled from him, and were sore afraid. (1 Samuel 17: 23–24 KJV)

This is the plan of God. This is God's expectation that he might present to himself a glorious church. God is looking to present to himself a glorious church. When we have a church without a shout of the king, we cannot call that a glorious church. It is a mob; a gathering, or a congregation of religious people. Jesus is not preparing for that. The characteristic of God's church is that she is simply glorious, there is no defeat, fear, or intimidation in their vocabulary or experience. In fact, the world will have a respite if the glorious church is taken to heaven because the glorious church has continuously tormented the enemy.

Christ is not coming for a church bandaged with bruises, on a stretcher, trying to breathe in an intensive care unit. He is not coming for a church that is dying and partially awake, or slumbering.

He is not coming for a church that already has a fat belly because of too much cake and coffee. He is not coming for a dancer's group or for those who have converted the temple into a place where they double money (prosperity gospel). He's coming for a glorious church without spot, without blemish, and without wrinkle. The identity we have in the spirit realm is an indication of our preparedness for the coming of Christ. There is an assault that Satan has been launching against the body of Christ to remove our identity, and then we look like civilians. And God cannot roar among us because we do not look like Him. He's coming for a bride. He is not coming for servants; He is coming for His bride because He is the bridegroom with a special fragrance.

Because of the imminence of Christ's coming, there is no more room for gambling, and testing ideologies and opinions. We have no more room for unnecessary debates on philosophies and psychologies of life prepared by the human mind. God is looking for a glorious church that will so torment the devil, wicked ones, and our civilization, that when Jesus eventually comes, the age, the world, sinners, will heave a sigh of relief, and they will say, thank goodness that they have gone for good. But do you know that if Jesus comes today, the world may not know because there's no difference between the church and the world? We are not tormenting the rulers of darkness in this age. A lion that does not roar is neither the strongest in the forest nor the strongest among the beasts. A lion that does not roar is afraid and ashamed. But there will be an emergence of warriors because God is going to unleash a battalion, an army of the Lord.

The king's wrath is as the roaring of a lion; but his favour is as dew upon the grass. (Proverbs 19:12 KJV)

When God is angry, He roars. God's anger must be heard against the works of darkness. It's like the roaring of a lion. That was why he roared against Pharaoh when Pharaoh refused to let the people of God go. The men of Israel did not allow God to roar through them, but David allowed God. They were afraid of Goliath, but David did understand that God hates provocation. David understood that God was angry at the wicked. Many of us have missed out. Many of us have not allowed God to roar through us because of our fears, timidity, and lack of understanding.

He hath not beheld iniquity in Jacob, neither hath he seen perverseness in Israel: the LORD his God is with him, and the shout of a king is among them. (Numbers 23:21 KJV)

This means that God shouts and roars. God is angry when the body of Christ is being ravaged by Jezebels. God is angry when Satan is taking men captive in our world. God is angry when darkness subdues light. God is angry and wants to roar through us. We must be people who allow God to roar against the wickedness in our lands, just as Jehu allowed God to roar against the witchcraft of Jezebel, thereby bringing judgment upon her and her false prophets.

Army against army.

For Israel and the Philistines had put the battle in array, army against army. And David left his carriage in the hand of the keeper of the carriage, and ran into the army, and came and saluted his brethren. And as he talked with them, behold, there came up the champion, the Philistine of Gath, Goliath by name, out of the armies of the Philistines, and spake according to the same words: and David heard them. And all the men of Israel, when they saw the man, fled from him, and were sore afraid. (1 Samuel 17: 21–24 KJV)

Do we see a transition here? In verse 21 a battle line was drawn. What kind of battle was that? It was an army of light positioned against the army of darkness. This approach appears glorious. However, Satan does not play fair, because he always fights every hour and every day, since he is acutely aware of his short time. Little wonder the Holy Ghost communicated to us by revelation that we also have a short time. As a result of Satan's seemingly brief spell on earth, he has devastated the world with his armies of demons and wicked spirits. On the other hand, we are believers, the arch-enemy of Satan. We are supposed to pitch our warfare as armies against armies, but, unfortunately, believers are pitching themselves as civilians against armies. What a shame! Hence, the disheartening defeat experienced by many Christians today.

When the church was born in the Acts of the Apostles, it was an army of apostles and evangelists led by Peter, James, Paul, Stephen, and Philip. They collided with forces of darkness and plummeted Satan's kingdom. God is interested in raising battalions that will challenge the decadence and the unrighteousness of this age.

A tragic change of regalia: from soldiers to civilians.

And David left his carriage in the hand of the keeper of the carriage, and ran into the army, and came and saluted his brethren. And as he talked with them, behold, there came up the champion, the Philistine of Gath, Goliath by name, out of the armies of the Philistines, and spake according to the same words: and David heard them. And all the men of Israel, when they saw the man, fled from him, and were sore afraid. (1 Samuel 17:22–24 KJV)

They were described as men. What a tragedy! When David ran into the army, he ran with confidence, belief, and assurance that he was running into the custodians of power, particularly, toward the stronghold of his nation's military. But when he arrived and Goliath showed up, the Israeli armies became men, and they ran in great panic. Does this indicate a change of regalia? In a moment, the identity of the army was converted to civilians. Even though they still retain their barracks, they've lost their capability as armies; they could no longer fight. This was their predicament for 40 days, whilst Goliath or "Go-Lion" kept roaring. Goliath seemed to perfectly understand the strategy for prosecuting such psychological disarmament. Goliath kept roaring, give me a man that will come and fight me.

The armies of Israel were physically numbered as armies, but they were spiritually impotent. They had lost their regalia. They were no longer known in the spirit realm as armies. Their title and ranks remained lieutenants, generals, captains, e.t.c, but they did not have capabilities in the spirit. They still had some physical weapons degraded potency, leaving them fully exposed to an unprecedented defeat.

It's time to put off the ineffective armaments of King Saul.

And Saul armed David with his armour, and he put an helmet of brass upon his head; also he armed him with a coat of mail. And David girded his sword upon his armour, and he assayed to go; for he had not proved it. And David said unto Saul, I cannot go with these; for I have not proved them. And David put them off him.
(1 Kings 17:38,39 KJV)
But the king has been in the cave for 40 days, and none of his armaments could withstand the words of Goliath. Now Saul thought it wise and nice to fortify David with something that has made him powerless. You see, that is the kind of advice we receive from parents, ancestors, church leaders, pastors, great men, and people that we go to for counsel. We go to them and they arm us with their own coat of mail. They stuff our heads with information that did not

deliver them in their own battles. They have not confronted the Goliath of their days. They managed to push the Goliaths to the next generation, and they are giving us the same tools that made them failures on the battlefield.

King Saul didn't know that none of these armaments was relevant when David confronted the lion in the forest. David was only wearing his normal native clothes and he said *I have not proven this*. King Saul's regalia might represent denominational, theological, family-based, cultural, societal, or religious and institutional clothing; which might be a recipe for disaster if devoid of the glory of God.

Verse 29 says, *"And David put them off him."* Every ideology we have acquired, every thought process, way of thinking, and accumulated artifacts that have been delivered to us from our parents, lineage, church members, and denominational group who are not free from addictions and sins needs to be put off completely to avoid defeat in life's battles.

Notes

Chapter 16
Accurately diagnosing the enemy's roar

And David spake to the men that stood by him, saying, What shall be done to the man that killeth this Philistine, and taketh away the reproach from Israel? for who is this uncircumcised Philistine, that he should defy the armies of the living God? And the people answered him after this manner, saying, So shall it be done to the man that killeth him. And Eliab his eldest brother heard when he spake unto the men; and Eliab's anger was kindled against David, and he said, Why camest thou down hither? and with whom hast thou left those few sheep in the wilderness? I know thy pride, and the naughtiness of thine heart; for thou art come down that thou mightest see the battle. And David said, What have I now done? Is there not a cause? (1 Samuel 17:26–29 KJV)

We have learned from the testimony of David how he was in the forest when the lion and the bear came to steal away the lamb. We have read David's testimony when the lion came to steal a lamb. We have learned that David was able to attack the lion and the bear because he was not sleeping at that time. A sleepy man cannot fight physically. David was watchful persistently and permanently. After the first victory against the lion, he did not throw away the skill of watchfulness and began to dance around and posting his victory on social media platforms. Whenever God gives you a victory, that is not the time to throw away your spiritual skill of watchfulness, because another battle might be lurking around the corner. Do you know that it is a tragedy to have a victory once, and the next time you have a defeat? It is better to have defeat earlier and then victory next. It might be devastating if we cannot sustain our victory because of a lack of watchfulness. If there is anything we must ingrain in our spirit, it is the skill of watchfulness. Let us learn to endure our joys.

And as he talked with them, behold, there came up the champion, the Philistine of Gath, Goliath by name, out of the armies of the Philistines, and spake according to the same words: and David heard them. (1 Samuel 17:23 KJV)

When David asked his brother about their situation, he heard a roar. This time around, it was not the roar of a lion in the forest, neither was it the roar of a beast nor of a bear in the bush; it was the roar of a lion-like man, Goliath of Gath. And the Bible tells us, *"For if the trumpet give an uncertain sound, who shall prepare himself to the battle?"* (1 Corinthians 14:8 KJV).

That means that it is not enough for us to be watchmen. We should have the capability to interpret what we are seeing or hearing. Many times, the Holy Ghost shows us a vision, and we misinterpret our vision, and then we end up in defeat. When David was on the battlefield, he heard Goliath's shout and tried to understand it in the best way possible. He said, *"And David spake to the men that stood by him, saying, What shall be done to the man that killeth this Philistine, and taketh away the reproach from Israel? for who is this uncircumcised Philistine, that he should defy the armies of the living God?"* (1 Samuel 17:26 KJV).

Importantly, David had just arrived at the battlefield and was not aware of the several events that had occurred on the battlefield in the previous 40 days. David interpreted this Goliath's peculiar sound blast as a reproach and an insult to Israel. David said, What should we do to the person who will take this mockery away? It was only

Goliath's voice that he heard in addition to the escape of the generals—the running away in fear of the generals—that he saw. But he interpreted this phenomenon as a reproach against Israel. Not only that, he continued, and said, what shall be done to this man who is defying the armies of the living God?

Do you know that the way we interpret what we see determines how we approach battles in life? As soon as David received the signal and the stimulus for which he made his conclusion, he did not go back to check if his conclusion was correct. David did not entertain any shadow of doubt on the conclusion that he had made that the name of God has been reproached. David did not begin to consider his age, size, and experience in warfare based on the conclusion that he has made, whether his personality, and his experience were capable of launching an attack. Do you know that because of the conclusion that David made, his language changed? Before now, David's language had been that of salutation. But when David made a watchman's conclusion, he stopped greeting people. The only thing he kept saying was, what shall be done to the man who kills this Philistine?

When David said, how can this reproach be taken away? He drew the anger of his elder brothers and his own family began verbally attacking him. His people started to talk about him as a proud man. And David responded to them, is there not a cause? Maybe his brethren wanted him to continue saluting them in their spiritual coma, and imminent defeat, but David had reached another conclusion. He had received a different stimulus, and immediately his mandate changed to following the main track of the heavenly Father. When we follow God like this, we will draw the hatred of people towards us. But this is a good thing; what happened to David was a sign that victory was near. His brothers had no idea that the solution to their 40-day embarrassment was already there on the battlefield.

Do you know that you are the one that God has chosen to bring a solution to the embarrassment in the body of Christ? And men are trying to ridicule you. People are looking at your size, financial ability, intelligence level, and your educational status. And they are using that to size you up. My friend, *"Greater is he that is in you, than he that is in the world"* (1 John 4:4 KJV).

The current predicament of the church of Christ.

The church Jesus spoke about is not a physical church but a divine army that is powerful enough to take the battle to the enemy's gates. These are not kindergarten babies, toddlers, or children who have not mastered the skill of handling spiritual weapons. These are not the children in the daycare center or anyone else who lacked skill in using spiritual weapons. When we look at our civilization and environment today, how do we classify the denominations and the local churches? Do they have the capability to wrestle against the gate of hell? Does it seem that they have the strength to fight against hell? Here, we see so many grown-up spiritual babies with feeding bottles, still crying for toys, and they have not come to the reality that the primary assignment of the church is to prevail against the gate of hell. They are still little kids eating from tin cans who cannot fight against hell. It's time for the body of Christ to awaken to a sense of responsibility and put on strength for the battle of the century.

Notes

Chapter 17
With God standing by, any lion can be defeated

And David said unto Saul, Thy servant kept his father's sheep, and there came a lion, and a bear, and took a lamb out of the flock: And I went out after him, and smote him, and delivered it out of his mouth: and when he arose against me, I caught him by his beard, and smote him, and slew him. (1 Samuel 17:34–35 KJV)

It is impossible for a boy, a teenager, to undertake such an unprecedented, risky mission by his natural strength. It must have been that an unseen person instigated and supported him. It is written that *no man can do these miracles that thou doest, except God be with him* (John 3:2b KJV). There was a time when Nehemiah was building the wall of Jerusalem, and Sanballat and Tobiah persistently harassed him, "You can't build this wall; you can't achieve this project. We are going to scatter it. Come over here." And they were threatening him. And Nehemiah said, *"Should such a man as I flee?"* (Nehemiah 6:11 KJV).

It is very easy to run away in times of problems, but those that stand in times of challenges—either financial, marital, emotional, stock market, or business crisis—do not stand because they found an intelligent way to navigate the crisis. No, they stand because they recognize someone standing behind them. In David's life, we understood that our decisions in life, responses to challenges, the spectacle of our eyes, and how we confront life's issues depend on who is standing by us.

David did not fortify himself with wealthy people, high-ranking generals in the army, or palace chiefs. Rather, David fortified himself with the presence of God. This is critical to our movement in the spirit realm, and to our development, victory, and signs and wonders. To address the lions of life, God must be on the voyage and we must be standing alongside Elohim because He is *"a present help in time of trouble"* (Psalms 46:1). We need to refocus all our plans, purposes, and projects on the person who is standing by us. If our greatest confidant and inner strength lies in the arena of the flesh, psychology, and philosophy we cannot stand the lion's roar.

David chose to make a decision: *"I went out after him."* That decision was predicated upon a reality—the consciousness of the person standing by him. Does this apply to you? Are there things you wish should be accomplished? Are there battles you are fighting? Are there things that you do not understand? It depends upon who is standing by you. The battles of life cannot be fought with our intelligence, with our experience, or with what we think we know. The reality is that if the Lord stands by us, every battle can be won. Because Paul made us realize, *"And the Lord shall deliver me from every evil work, and will preserve me unto his heavenly kingdom: to whom be glory for ever and ever. Amen."* (2 Timothy 4:18 KJV).

Jonathan was faced with an uphill task of subduing an enemy and his battalion consisted of himself and his armour bearer only. Jonathan said it is nothing with God to save by many or by few. The enemies thought that they would easily extinguish them since they were only two fighters. But Jonathan understood that the Lord was with them. They attacked their enemies and obtained a tremendous result (see 1 Samuel 14). Should we not think that the greatest asset that we can possess today is the presence of the Lord? Moses said, *"And he said unto him, If thy presence go not with me, carry us not up hence."* (Exodus 33:15 KJV).

What does it take for God to stand by us?

And God said unto Jacob, Arise, go up to Bethel, and dwell there: and make there an altar unto God, that appeared unto thee when thou fleddest from the face of Esau thy brother. Then Jacob said unto his household, and to all that were with him, Put away the strange gods that are among you, and be clean, and change your garments: And let us arise, and go up to Bethel; and I will make there an altar unto God, who answered me in the day of my distress, and was with me in the way which I went. And they gave unto Jacob all the strange gods which were in their hand, and all their earrings which were in their ears; and Jacob hid them under the oak which was by Shechem. And they journeyed: and the terror of God was upon the cities that were round about them, and they did not pursue after the sons of Jacob. (Genesis 35 1–5 KJV)

What does it take for the Lord to stand by us? The answer is in this passage. First, God came to Jacob and said, I want to fight for you, but I cannot fight for you because there is sin in your camp, there is uncleanness and evil amongst you. Go to Bethel. Immediately, Jacob remembered what Bethel was. It was a place of divine visitation, a place where heaven and earth combined to produce revelation, insight, and glory. Bethel was the location where a ladder connected heaven with earth and angels ascended and descended. It is a place where God's voice is audible. And God told Jacob, If you want such an experience, you have to find that place again. And Jacob called his entire family and preached to them.

And Jacob knew this was a place of prayer; this was a place where God dwells. It is better to relocate to God's abode. For many years, he had pursued riches and wealth, but he became a big man with big trouble because enemies were pursuing him and angry at his wealth. His life was at stake and that of his family, and his children were at risk of being slaughtered by lions. Thus, Jacob called his entire household and told them that there was a consecration that brought His presence. Jacob instructed his family to put away strange gods, idols, desires, appetites, longings, and strange interactions. God cannot stand with us when all these negative things are found in our lives.

Jacob was mighty, yet his family was corrupt. Jacob was blessed with all the riches of this earth, and yet his family members were unclean and were serving idols. There were strange ideologies and concepts among them. They've corrupted themselves with the cares of this life. The appearance of the world and the church should not be the same. The disposition, songs, and music of the world should not find their way into the church of God. What are our interests? Do we dance to the rock stars in the world, and thereafter also sing praise and worship before God? Something is wrong. God cannot stand by you. Consider the ungodly people in the world—how they dress, how they talk, the kinds of parties they go to, and how they drink. As a believer, do you drink like them, dress like them, think and talk like them, and participate in the things they do? If yes, the presence of the Lord cannot be with you; leaving you to the mercies of rampaging lions of this life.

Wherefore come out from among them, and be ye separate, saith the Lord, and touch not the unclean thing; and I will receive you, And will be a Father unto you, and ye shall be my sons and daughters, saith the Lord Almighty. (2 Corinthians 6:17,18 KJV)

Our generation is so free from the lack of separation from the world. The Holy Ghost departed from many local churches a long time ago. Why? Because the church brought in strange idols. We have now begun to merchandise the house of God. Even though God was blessing Jacob, it was a blessing that was predicated upon the covenant God had with Abraham, not a blessing associated with Jacob himself. And God said, *I don't want you to remain at that level; there is yet another dimension. If only you could go back to Bethel, where I met you.* And Jacob agreed that it was a better choice to have the presence of God in his life than to enjoy the blessings of sin for a season.

God spoke to Jacob; God told him that he needed to dwell there in Bethel. That is, you do not go there and stay for two minutes, and then run back into the world. Well, after tasting that God is good in Bethel, you cannot return to the ways you used to think, the books you used to read, the pornographic and lust-filled videos you previously watched, the tendencies and corruptions of the flesh. Jacob said there is something about Bethel. He said, *"And let us arise, and go up to Bethel; and I will make there an altar unto God, who answered me in the day of my distress."*

Do you know that if we pay attention to the times when we were in distress, those were the times when we were very close to God? Those were the times when we were living a life of consecration and self-denial. In times of need, when we had nothing and were empty of resources, we had tremendous amounts of pain and trouble, and we didn't even know where the next meal would come from. Those were the times that we achieved the highest level of consecration, and now that we are wealthy, now that we are satisfied, now that we are rich, we have forgotten the altar of the living God and we have turned back to the affairs of this life.

Love not the world, neither the things that are in the world. If any man love the world, the love of the Father is not in him. (1 John 2:15 KJV)

You cannot love the world and love God at the same time; they are mutually exclusive. The presence of God will never be with people who love the world and try to erect a strange altar. God is not there. Do you know that because Jacob responded to that great call, today we can talk about the God of Jacob, the God of Isaac, and the God of Abraham? When God revealed himself to Moses, He had to declare, "I am the God of Abraham, Isaac, and Jacob." God had to bring the name of this man into this realization. Why did that happen? Because he responded to the call.

It is not so much about the lion; it is so much about the presence of God with us. When the storms of life are raging, the Bible says, *"These things I have spoken unto you, that in me ye might have peace. In the world ye shall have tribulation: but be of good cheer; I have overcome the world."* (John 16:33 KJV). The presence of God with us is so much greater than the glories of this world. What is our pursuit? What has crept into our lives? Paul the Apostle said, *"For if I build again the things which I destroyed, I make myself a transgressor."* (Galatians 2:18 KJV).

"And they gave unto Jacob all the strange gods which were in their hand, and all their earrings which were in their ears." (Genesis 35:4 KJV). They heard the message and responded. Whenever the Holy Ghost calls a believer back to consecration, there should be a response. When there is a response at the human level, there will be a response at the divine level. Everybody brought their strange gods. The scripture kept referring to them as 'strange'. It is strange because God does not know them, strange idols because God does not know them, strange things because God did not approve of them. What are the strange idols that have crept into your life? Either by

cultural practice, denominational affiliation, experiences of people, suggestions of friends and neighbors, strange board games, video games, magazines, or fashion that is coming into your life. The Holy Ghost is saying, Arise, go to Bethel and dwell there; make an altar unto God there.

Oh believer, return to your times of fasting and prayers, the days of your consecration, and the depth of commitment. Return to the study of the scriptures and to worship so that you can carry Bethel everywhere you go.

And they gave unto Jacob all the strange gods which were in their hand, and all their earrings which were in their ears; (Genesis 35:4KJV)

Jacob did not particularly mention their earrings. He only said, change your garments. These people understood the message so deeply that they realized that the presence of God could not go with them with their earrings. The earrings are a language that connotes bondage and perpetual slavery (Exodus 21:1-6 and Exodus 33:5,6).

Now these are the ordinances you [Moses] shall set before [the Israelites]. If you buy a Hebrew servant [as the result of debt or theft], he shall serve six years, and in the seventh he shall go out free, paying nothing. If he came [to you] by himself, he shall go out by himself; if he came married, then his wife shall go out with him. If his master has given him a wife and she has borne him sons or daughters, the wife and her children shall be her master's, and he shall go out [of your service] alone. But if the servant shall plainly say, I love my master, my wife, and my children; I will not go free, Then his master shall bring him to God [the judges as His agents]; he shall bring him to the door or doorpost and **shall pierce his** *ear with an awl; and he shall serve him for life.* Exodus 21:1-6 AMPC

When the people heard these stern words, they went into mourning and stripped themselves of their jewelry and ornaments. For the Lord had told Moses to tell them, "You are an unruly, stubborn people. If I were there among you for even a moment, I would exterminate you. **Remove your jewelry and ornaments until I decide what to do with you."** *So, after that, they wore no jewelry.* Exodus 33:4-6 Living bible

The Bible says, where the spirit of God is, there is liberty. God does not want to see an emblem of spiritual bondage. The people of Israel began to bring down every pillar, altar, and identity that connotes bondage, evil, and uncleanness out of their lives. Jacob gathered everything, and the Bible says that he buried them under a tree. And after that consecration was completed, they began to journey.

And they journeyed: and the terror of God was upon the cities that were round about them, and they did not pursue after the sons of Jacob.

God is not under any obligation to create terror for our enemies if our lives repel him. Therefore God is calling us to a high degree of holiness through separation and consecration unto Him. Civilization may change, and how people understand things may change, but the word of God is yea and amen. *For ever, O LORD, thy word is settled in heaven.* (Psalm 119:89 KJV)

If we want to experience what David experienced before the lion and the bear, we must live a consecrated life. If we want to experience what Jacob experienced, we must put all these ungodly things out of our lives. We must put away everything that does not enable us to be identified first by the glory of God. It is the glory of the flesh we that must put away, and then we will begin to enjoy the terror of the Lord on the kingdom of darkness.

Notes

Chapter 18
Testimony qualifies us to face Goliath or Golion, but the brook provides the weapons to defeat him

And he took his staff in his hand, and chose him five smooth stones out of the brook, and put them in a shepherd's bag which he had, even in a scrip; and his sling was in his hand: and he drew near to the Philistine. And the Philistine came on and drew near unto David; and the man that bare the shield went before him. And when the Philistine looked about, and saw David, he disdained him: for he was but a youth, and ruddy, and of a fair countenance. And the Philistine said unto David, Am I a dog, that thou comest to me with staves? And the Philistine cursed David by his gods.
(1 Samuel 17:40–43 KJV)

A teenager called David, fought the enemy after he had physically overcome all the challenges in Israel. These included the challenges of coming before the king, his elder brothers' reprimand, cultural setbacks, and the traditions of his time that say, you cannot go to war unless you have submitted yourself to the school of theology, combat training school, and learnt how to use the spear and the sword. He overcame all hurdles because he was not naturally qualified, but his testimony qualified him. His testimony was special because none of the generals in the Israeli army at that time had such testimonies. They had the weapons, they had the strategy, yet they also had the defeat. This man did not have the weapon or the strategy, but he had the testimony that he was victorious.

He was now alone, faced with the strategic enemy, the Goliath of Gath. Importantly, the things needed to have a victory over his people were not the same things he needed to fight Goliath. He needed testimony to qualify him to fight Goliath, but he didn't need testimony to fight Goliath himself; he needed something else. He needed testimony to convince Saul to approve of him going against Goliath. Our testimony gives us an advantage to stand against the enemy. But we also need something beyond our testimony; our testimony alone may not be sufficient. Our testimonies may qualify us and bring us an opportunity that no one else has experienced. Your testimony may place you in an advantageous position where you are qualified for certain promises and glory. But for us to walk in the reality of this glory, we might need something else.

David went to work. What work did he do? He went to the river. And we know by the Spirit of God that the water is the Holy Ghost.

He that believeth on me, as the scripture hath said, out of his belly shall flow rivers of living water. (But this spake he of the Spirit, which they that believe on him should receive: for the Holy Ghost was not yet given; because that Jesus was not yet glorified. (John 7:38,39 KJV)

He went to the river and he chose five smooth stones. He could have gone to the forest and looked for stones there. But there is a special design and architecture the stones at the riverside provide. Similarly, in this dispensation, there is a strategy that only the Holy Ghost can inspire; there is a weaponization that only the Holy Ghost can impart. As mighty as the testimonies were to qualify David for war, the testimony still left him handicapped of the implement he needed to bring Goliath down. In verse 48 of 1 Samuel 17, David drew near to the Philistines when he was so sure his stones were in his bag, and his sling was intact, he was acutely ready to face the champion of Gath also called *"GO-LION" that roars.*

It will be a disaster to go towards the Philistines without gathering the tools that the Holy Ghost has set aside. Let us not be in a rush. Let us spend more time accumulating the stones for this victory by the riverside, by the brooding process of the Holy Ghost, by cultivating fellowship with the Holy Spirit. And as we cultivate communion with Him by the riverside, He will begin to inspire and impart into our spiritman all the stones necessary to take down Goliath in our lives, in the nation, and in the lives of other people.

Notes

Chapter 19
Breaking the teeth of lions (Goliath's curse)

And the Philistine said unto David, Am I a dog, that thou comest to me with staves? And the Philistine cursed David by his gods. And it came to pass, when the Philistine arose, and came, and drew nigh to meet David, that David hastened, and ran toward the army to meet the Philistine. (1 Samuel 17:43,48 KJV)

For 40 days. a man rendered the entire army of Israel incapacitated; they were powerless. They were turned from armies to men because somebody was busy roaring somewhere, and with every roar for each passing day, the voice was diminishing the strength of the entire army of Israel. Every roar was reducing generals into captains and captains into civilians. Every roar of Goliath *(GO-LION)* was causing trepidation.

What was in this roar? What was in this talk? What was he saying? What could make those men who the entire nation is looking up to and depending upon to keep them away from captivity suddenly begin to tremble? Remember, Goliath had not killed one person. Goliath had not even applied his sword. Goliath had not shot a single arrow. He was only speaking, and for 40 days, Israel could not even throw a stone. It is to tell us that fundamentally, **the battles of life are purely in the spirit realm. The physical realm is the theater of manifestation. And whosoever gains ascendancy in the spirit will manifest victory in the physical realm.** And all Israel had were physical implements; the man who was in charge in the spirit of darkness, Goliath, was speaking, and there was no response from Israel.

The spirit realm is charged with warfare; arrows are flying everywhere, and we, as a body of Christ, have become victims of this warfare. Why? Because we are not praying in the Holy Ghost. Because we only think with our minds. We think everything is just simply what we can see, hear, and feel. No, it's much more than that. The Bible says that when Goliath saw that finally, after 40 days, somebody emerged from the conclave of fear, somebody emerged from the conclave of defeat, from the conclave of intimidation, from the darkness of decay, and his name was David and he looked so small, tiny, and so feeble.

Goliath thought that if there was a possibility that a tiny creature could emerge out of this impossibility, and colossal crumbling of the Israeli army, if there was a possibility that a human being after 40 days could come out and say he wanted to fight me, then I know that person is not ordinary, and so, quickly, Goliath referred the case to the spiritual realm.

Look at how many times we, as believers, take things for granted and people like Goliath don't. Goliath had his weapons; his armor bearer had his weapons; the Philistines' host were at his back; yet none of those things had any significance to Goliath except the spirit realm, where he had to configure the battle by cursing with his gods. Has it occurred to you that when you choose to rise out of the darkness of your civilization, when you choose to break even out of your family line that has been under the tutelage of year-long defeat, when you decide to pray, there is resistance; that is the Goliath of Gath? Have you understood that when the enemy sees that you are trying to make a move that is different from what is customary among your people, there is resistance? What do you do?

Goliath placed a curse on David. Goliath began to invoke spirits that would paralyze David with fear. The Bible did not tell us details of his incantations, but I tell you that Goliath communicated with Satan. That was why David's response was to communicate with God and bring God as his 7-star defense system. It was a battle of gods; the physical realm was second to that. The Bible says that when David sprang out of that conclave of intimidation and volunteered to fight, Goliath saw him. Goliath said, Am I a dog? That means Goliath saw what David had in his hands. But Goliath did not see that David didn't only bring a catapult but went to the river for stones.

Goliath did not see that David went to the river of the Holy Ghost. This is so important in waging spiritual warfare. You know this one is an atypical battle because the last time David fought, he fought with a physical lion. he didn't need a brook/river. He fought a bear, he didn't need a brook nor need a catapult. He didn't need a stone because the level of anointing he had was enough to destroy physical lions; physical lions do not consult an oracle; they do not curse because they can not speak. But when it comes to another general called Goliath and his warfare, antics, and abilities, plus his ability to reinforce himself with supernatural dimensions, then David had a realization. I cannot go with my salvation experience alone, nor my sanctification experience alone. Those experiences were enough for the lion and the bear, I needed the baptism in the Holy Ghost. So, he went into the river.

David went into the brook, and he got himself stones (strategies) that he put in his bag, and with that, he was confident. Why did he do that? Because David realized something: that this army of King Saul was under a curse. How do you think he knew? He knew this because of the direction that they always took whenever Goliath asked for somebody to come and fight.

A curse is an atmosphere that gives us a negative direction—reverse gear.

That was why Goliath knew that anyone who would make an attempt to come forward had broken the curse. And that person is not normal. All of Israel and its army were always running backward. When Goliath roared, the whole army and king Saul were hiding in the cave. Only Goliath could move forward because he was in charge. The Bible tells us that when Goliath saw David, he began to speak in his own incantation, that is, in his own *other tongues*, so to speak. He quickly switched into the spirit realm, and when he did that, David immediately entered the spirit realm. Why? Because he was capable. Why is he capable? He was just coming from the river.

It is not about the length of the curse; it is not about the magnitude of the curse. It is not about how many years the curse has been following you. It is not about who made the pronouncement. It is much more about where you are coming from. If you are coming from the river, you are up to the task. If you are coming from the Holy Ghost, you are up to the task. Have you lost one property or another? Have you lost money? Have people disappointed you? And you are coming under an influence like a shadow of darkness coming upon you. Begin to pray in the Spirit and liberate yourself. Begin to pray in the Spirit right now, right now, that darkness will turn to light.

The Bible says, to the surprise of the Philistines, in verse 48, Goliath rose up because he thought he was in charge. After he placed the curse, he was expecting the same movement to happen to David, namely, to run backward. He was expecting that David would practically lose all his acceleration and begin to decelerate. He was expecting that the coordinates would change from north to south and that David would turn backward 180 degrees. After placing a curse in the atmosphere, he was thinking about immobilization, thinking that David would be so hypnotized, immobilized, ostracized, and disabled that he could not make any progress forward. To his surprise, when he got up and began to come against what he called a dog-boy, he realized that the so-called dog-boy was running towards him. Goliath was first of all embarrassed; he was shocked that his curse did not work. The boy is running forward. Before he could finish processing his thoughts, something landed on his forehead. He was on the ground.

Notes

Chapter 20
Goliath/Golion is dead

For us to prevail and to fulfill our destiny, which is the key, we need to overcome Goliath. Goliath was part of the assignment David needed to overcome to fulfill his destiny. Goliath's primary aim was to make sure that these people of God became servants.

And it came to pass, when the Philistine arose, and came and drew nigh to meet David, that David hasted, and ran toward the army to meet the Philistine. (1 Samuel 17:48 KJV)

The moment the Philistine arose and charged towards David, that was the defining moment. There was no turning back in this situation. The Bible says, *"David hasted, and ran toward the army to meet the Philistine."* David knew that this time around his life was no longer in his hands. David knew that this time of his survival was dependent on the fact that he arose and ran towards the Philistine. You don't wait for the Philistine to come and meet you. Ah, that means you have lost balance because he will strike you when you turn your back. When he comes and you allow him to gravitate towards you, he's going to map out where you are, and your coordinates, figure out the direction of your escape, and then negotiate a disaster for you. You don't wait for the enemy to rise and come and meet you. Rather, you run toward the enemy, and to run, you need supernatural strategic stamina that you have gotten by the river *(Holy Ghost)*.

The Philistine was not going toward the people of Israel because he knew that for 40 days they had been ostracized. He must have said within himself that *this tiny fellow, David, who came to talk to me, seems to have a certain level of stamina. I need to quench it. I need to break his backbone.* So he rose. But you know, when David was running towards the Philistine, he didn't have Goliath in mind, rather he had the entire Philistine army in mind. To get to the army, you need to step over the champion, Goliath. David wanted to show the world that there is a God in Israel. My friend, do you think you have a problem? Perhaps, you don't. Because that problem is your stepping stone to announce to the world that God is still with his children.

After David had put his hand in his bag, remember that the bag was still very wet with the water from the brook. The stone he picked was still very wet with the water of the brook. He slung it and smote it, and the stone sank into the forehead of the Philistine. The last verse, the last sentence in verse 49 says, "And *he fell upon his face to the earth."*

The Philistine was facing David but did not fall backward. That means Goliath died when the stone arrived in his skull. The trajectory of the stone should have naturally tilted his fall backward. That means he completely lost consciousness as soon as the stone impacted him. We could safely conclude that since Goliath fell forward, it means he died before he fell.

Therefore David ran, and stood upon the Philistine, and took his sword, and drew it out of the sheath thereof, and slew him, and cut off his head therewith. And when the Philistines saw their champion was dead, they fled. (1 Samuel 17:51 KJV)

David did not give the army of the Philistines time to conceive a different explanation of what was going on. He ran and quickly demonstrated to them that, *look, your champion is dead.* We must keep running. David ran. As he was running, God was preparing Goliath as his foot mat. Oh he became a foot mat; he fell with his face to the ground! The Bible says that *death and life are in the power of the tongue: and they that love it shall eat the fruit thereof.* (Proverbs 18:21 KJV)

All humans by default have a Goliath which is sin whose wages is death. Jesus Christ came from heaven and died on the cross to destroy the power of sin, satan, and death. It is non-negotiable to have this victory first by accepting Jesus as your Lord and Saviour. *The last enemy that shall be destroyed is death.* (1 Corinthians 15:26 KJV).

Since, therefore, [these His] children share in flesh and blood [in the physical nature of human beings], He [Himself] in a similar manner partook of the same [nature], that by [going through] death He might bring to nought and make of no effect him who had the power of death—that is, the devil—And also that He might deliver and completely set free all those who through the [haunting] fear of death were held in bondage throughout the whole course of their lives. (Hebrews 2:14,15 AMPC).

Now we invite you to defeat the greatest Goliath of life which is sin. Kindly say this prayer and mean it from the bottom of your heart.

> *Dear Lord Jesus Christ, I believe you are the Son of God who died on the cross for my sins. I believe you rose again for my salvation. I acknowledge that I am a sinner, please forgive my sins, have mercy on me, wash my heart clean with your precious blood, I repent of all my evil lifestyle, sins, addictions, and habits. Please come into my heart, write my name in your heavenly book and give me the joy of Salvation. I*

believe in my heart what I now confess with my mouth, that I am a child of God. Amen, Halleluyah, Glory be to God.

Arise in prayers and begin to announce that every enemy pursuing your family, finances, ministry, health, and soul is dead; every wickedness of the wicked pursuing you is dead. Amen, Halleluyah.

       GOLIATH / GO-LION is dead!

Should you have testimonies, prayer requests, and questions based on this book, please contact us via:

flamethefreeze@gmail.com

WhatsApp +358 46 571 4634

www.flamethefreeze.com

A free e-copy of the book ***Flame the Freeze*** can be downloaded on the website.

www.ingramcontent.com/pod-product-compliance
Lightning Source LLC
Chambersburg PA
CBHW061220070526
44584CB00029B/3914